ADVERTISING AGENCY AND STUDIO SKILLS

ILLUSTRATED BY THE AUTHOR

ADVERTISING AGENCY AND STUDIO SKILLS

A GUIDE TO THE PREPARATION OF ART AND MECHANICALS FOR REPRODUCTION

by Tom Cardamone

REVISED AND ENLARGED EDITION

WATSON-GUPTILL PUBLICATIONS   NEW YORK

To Louise

First Edition

First Printing, 1959

Second Printing, 1961

Third Printing, 1964

Fourth Printing, 1967

Fifth Printing, 1968

Second Edition

First Printing, 1970

Second Printing, 1973

© 1970 by Watson-Guptill Publications
Published by Watson-Guptill Publications,
a division of Billboard Publications, Inc.
One Astor Plaza, New York, N.Y. 10036
Manufactured in U.S.A.
ISBN 0–8230–0150–4
Library of Congress Catalog Card Number: 74–125845

Foreword

Board procedure for artists in agencies and studios encompasses numerous skills and techniques. One category of this procedure is referred to as "mechanicals," which, although it is essentially a subject within itself, is yet so interrelated with all other aspects of board procedure, that it is difficult to define. Because the subject requires so vast a knowledge of advertising, it is fast becoming a necessary prerequisite to gaining a foothold in the broad field of advertising. Keen competition makes it difficult for the average student, at the onset of his career, to obtain his first position in the capacity he desires. There is little time to break in the beginner—he must already have some knowledge of the business, not just creative ability. In order to produce the desired effect, which is the result of advertising "know-how," the beginner must first accumulate certain specific information and experience.

While the student (as well as the already developed artist) is making every effort to find a position that will afford him an opportunity for self-expression, he must reach out in every direction for additional, more extensive knowledge and understanding, in order to nurture his latent creativity, as well as his manual capabilities.

Quite often, the man who does mechanicals is not considered a creative artist. He is sometimes looked upon as an ordinary machine operator in a factory. This attitude, of course, is fallacious. An employer may say, "Mechanical men? They're expendable." An experienced artist may say, "Mechanicals? There's nothing to it! You can learn it in two weeks." These men have either forgotten how long it takes to learn all the requirements of this position, or are kidding themselves into thinking they know all that it involves. For, if they deliberated the requirements of the artist as a mechanical man, they would realize that to achieve the true expertness of an all-round professional takes a good deal of experience and hard work. The artist must not only develop his manual dexterity, he must possess unlimited knowledge of advertising procedure. He is a technician as well as an artist, and his product, the mechanical, affords his employer a fair profit.

The increasing demand for good mechanical men (or board men) is becoming more apparent every day within our studios and agencies, owing to the growing realization of their importance. (For the sake of clarifying the distinction between the "mechanical man" and the "board man," you might consider the board man as being the more advanced, all-round professional artist of the two.) It is my purpose in writing this book not only to offer valuable information for the artist, but to acquaint the upper echelon with the qualifications of the professional mechanical and board man.

By and large, it is not necessary to possess any special artistic talent in order to learn mechanicals. Essentially, it is a manual technique used in conjunction with certain information. Naturally, the more knowledge and experience at his command, the more efficient the mechanical man will be. But there is one thing that separates the ordinary from the professional and that is *judgment* in the preparation of mechanicals. The artist's esthetic sense plays an important role in the development of good judgment. This is something that cannot be taught in a book—it must be developed through experience.

While the artist has much to offer mechanicals, it is fortunate that mechanicals offers more, in return, to the artist. During the process of learning this procedure, he is developing his skill in handling tools, equipment, and increasing his knowledge of advertising makeup; he is exposed to new areas of the advertising business. A thorough knowledge of mechanicals has enabled many artists to gain entrance into a variety of jobs in the advertising field. The extensive discipline mechanicals provides allows the artist trained in this area to choose from many different—and attractive—possibilities. He may not want to be an illustrator after all, or an art director's position may no longer appeal to him— he may have acquired an appetite for production or studio managing. Perhaps he would rather sell art than prepare it, or he might even start his own studio.

With the advance of methods and means, the business of advertising has become a many-faceted composite of esthetic, educated, progressive, and hard working men and women. Its energy is expended the world over. The artist as a mechanical man is an essential gear within this machinery, and without him production could not continue at its present volume.

This book represents an accumulation of information that would take considerable time at school and experience in the field to obtain. It is a foundation for the beginner and a source of further information for the already experienced artist, upon which can be built a pleasant and fruitful future in advertising.

However, the content of this book alone is not the answer to your future as an artist; rather, regard it as a vehicle for advancement toward creative expression. The development of these technical skills will enhance your opportunities for making a living, but this use of tools, material, and accumulation of technical knowledge should serve only as a medium for the construction of cultural contributions.

It isn't enough to be a competent technician in the art field, whether it be commercial or otherwise. The artist carries the responsibility of contributing to contemporary society. He must create and cultivate new meanings and formulas. He must broaden his scope of ethics and philosophy so that his graphic communication with the world may function as a nourishing influence toward its cultural development. Do not be content with having acquired manual dexterity or technical proficiency, but enthusiastically launch yourself into further studies in the related fields of graphic expression.

Contents

Introduction

In order that you may visualize the mechanical man's part in advertising make-up, I have briefly summarized the general steps taken to produce an advertisement in agencies and studios. They are as follows:

The client has a product to advertise.

He contacts the account executive at a particular advertising agency.

The account executive, in turn, confers with the copywriter, art director, or creative director.

The account man proposes his plan to the client and, after due consideration and approval, it is put into effect.

Copy is written for the client's approval.

The art director prepares layouts or roughs for client approval. In many cases, a more comprehensive layout is prepared.

After an o. k. from the client, the type is ordered, and usually the art director and account executive discuss (with the production manager) proper procedure for execution, according to budget and time.

The production manager confers with his platemakers and printers to estimate costs.

The artist (mechanical man) is given the layout, together with its mechanical instructions and components.

After the mechanical has been prepared, it may be sent back to the client for further consideration. If no changes are necessary, the mechanical is then sent to the platemaker.

After plates are made, three or four proofs are sent to the production manager for final checkup and possible change before printing the required quantity.

If the proofs meet with the approval of the production manager and everyone concerned, the printer completes the run.

Now that you know the position of the artist as a mechanical man, you can readily understand his importance and responsibility. To begin with, the advertisement cannot be produced without some sort of "mechanical art assembly" that corresponds with the layout. What appears in the mechanical will appear in final printing. Should there be an error (on anyone's part) in this mechanical, it could be quite costly. Therefore, it is the obligation of the mechanical man to see to it that all the requirements of the job are fulfilled with complete accuracy and understanding.

The work procedure described throughout this book is directed toward studio and agency operation dealing in high level work—*quality*, not *economy*. It is my contention that the artist who has been taught the execution of superior work will have no difficulty learning the cheaper, sometimes quicker, and less skillful approach. But the artist who starts his career in this lower echelon will go through a good deal of struggling to attain the upper level of quality.

1

Paste-ups

The paste-up man is usually an apprentice. His duties deal mostly with the preparation of dummies, mounting photos and art, cutting mats (frames) for art, pasting up assemblies for various presentations, etc. Generally, he has nothing to do with mechanicals.

A *paste-up mechanical* (or simply a mechanical) is art prepared in paste-up form, specifically for reproduction in strict accordance with a layout or dummy under the supervision of an art director.

LAYOUTS, DUMMIES, ART

An idea is conceived for an advertisement with specific conditions, and small, rough sketches, called *thumbnails,* are worked out in searching for an appropriate layout. Using the thumbnail as a guide, the art director will draw an actual size "layout" of his idea. The layout may either be roughly indicated or "worked-up" enough to present a fairly concise visual idea of the arrangement. A mechanical is made, using this layout as a guide.

Very often the client will want to see a more thorough visualization of the idea or layout. In such cases, with the layout as a guide, a comprehensive ("comp") is made. The comp looks as close to the finished printed job as possible. With this comp as a guide, the mechanical is made.

For folders, mailing pieces, brochures, etc., the actual piece is constructed by hand, according to the layout in comprehensive form, and presented to the client. This is called a "dummy," and it is also followed in the preparation of the mechanical.

"Art" does not necessarily mean a drawing or painting. Any finished piece that is to be used for reproduction is considered art. Many also refer to art as "copy."

Fig. 1 *T-square and triangle*

Fig. 2 *Push pins*

Fig. 3 *Dividers*

Fig. 5 *Ruling pen*

Fig. 7 *Ink (black, red, and blue)*

Fig. 6 *Crowquill pen*

Fig. 4 *Compass*

Fig. 8 *Brushes: nos. 1, 3, and 6*

Fig. 9 *Thinner dispenser*

Fig. 10 *Cotton*

Fig. 11 *Cement containers*

Fig. 12 *Sand block*

Fig. 13 *Water jars*

Fig. 14 *Thinner (solvent)*

Fig. 15 *Rubber cement*

Fig. 16 Template pen

Fig. 17 Kneaded eraser
and ink eraser

Fig. 18 Dust brush

Fig. 19 Tweezers

Fig. 20 Scissors,
utility knife,
and razor blades

Fig. 21 Palette

$\frac{1}{16}''$ $\frac{1}{8}''$ $\frac{1}{2}''$ $1''$

$\frac{1}{32}''$ $\frac{1}{4}''$

$\frac{3}{4}''$

Fig. 23 Ruler

Fig. 22 Masking tape

Fig. 24 French curve

Fig. 25 Plastic spray
and fixative

Fig. 26 Paint
(black and white)

Fig. 27 Pencils:
F, 3H, and 6H

Fig. 28 Thumbnail.

Fig. 29 Layout.

Fig. 30 The artwork is made
actual size in the dummy.

Fig. 31 The comp looks like the piece reproduced.

MATERIALS AND TOOLS

Because of the variety of work and problems encountered each day in advertising, there is actually no limit to the number and types of tools and equipment used. However, there are certain materials needed for the average, everyday job, without which the artist limits his capabilities. Illustrated here are such tools. Learn to know how and when to use them properly.

PAPER STOCK

Listed here are the papers and boards you will work with almost every day. There are others, but these are the most widely used:

Bond paper (ledger bond): a smooth, opaque, white paper. It comes in three weights: light, medium, and heavy. Bond may be used for line drawings, masks, flaps, dummies, and comprehensives.

Visual bond: a "toothy," translucent white paper used in preparing comps, layouts, and dummies.

Tracing paper: an almost transparent paper having unlimited uses, but mainly for layouts, color indications on art or mechanicals, flaps, slipsheets, etc.

Illustration board: available in a variety of makes, grades, and surfaces. Generally two types of surfaces will serve you: rough and smooth. Rough surface boards are used in mechanicals that do not require clean line inking, all types of finished art work, and comps. The smooth surface boards are used for mechanicals demanding smooth, clean line work, for many styles of finished art, for mounting photos or art, and for comps.

Strathmore (or other paper of similar quality): a paper produced in various weights, used for mechanicals, art work, and dummies.

Matboard (pebble board): also made in a variety of surfaces. However, it has its peculiarities. It is a soft, inferior grade of board and should be used with discretion. Do not mount a photo on pebble board, as it might leave a textured impression on the photo that may interfere with reproduction. Its main use is for matting (framing) art and layouts. It may be used for art work when a particular technique is sought. *Never* use pebble board for a mechanical.

Mounting board: usually smooth and of substantial weight. Used for mounting or backing up photos or art.

Color background paper: available in many brands, this is simply a sheet of paper colored on one side. Because it comes in a very wide range of hues and tints, it has untold uses.

Colorfilm sheets: for texture and color separation available in many brands, a clear acetate film, coated on one side with a thin, transparent, gelatin-type emulsion. This colored gelatin may be scraped away, exposing the clear film. There are two types of this paper: the adhesive backed and the nonadhesive. Available in many colors and tints, it is especially helpful in finished art and color separation on mechanicals. Because of its transparent quality, it presents an excellent visualization of the effects desired.

Screen or texture sheets (available in many brands): thin, clear acetate film having a "line" (black or white) texture or pattern printed on one side. Formerly known as Ben Day sheets, these have an adhesive backing. The sheet is placed onto a mechanical or art, and the desired shape is cut out and burnished. This is especially useful where "tone" effects are desired on "line" art. (*See Chapter 4.*)

Vellum: a heavy tracing paper used for tracing, art work, and in the preparation of overlays for color separation on mechanicals and art. Ink or paint can be scratched off with a razor blade for corrections and special effects.

Acetate: frosted or clear, available in different weights, used for color separation overlays and art. Ink can be scratched off for special effects or corrections.

LIGHT TABLE

Some artists just can not get along without a light table. While it is not an absolute necessity, it offers innumerable advantages. If you feel the cost of a commercial light table is beyond your present capacity, it is simple to make your own. You might try converting an old drawing table into one. This is very convenient. When not in use as a light table, place a board over it and use it as a drawing table. (Fig. 32.)

Fig. 32 Light table.

RAZOR BLADES

Razor blades do not retain their sharpness very long. As a matter of fact, one lasts long enough to cut only one mat. Always use a fresh blade when cutting something important. Caution: it is dangerous to manipulate elements during a paste-up (such as type) with the corner of the blade edge. The tip of the blade may snap off and fly in your face. If you must use a razor for this, try the corner of the back edge (single edged razor blade), but be careful or you may cut your finger.

POLAROID CAMERA

A polaroid camera is unquestionably useful in figure work as well as an aid in drawing objects or products. It is also used in the preparation of layouts or comps. You can photostat the polaroid print to suit your needs. This can be a tremendous time saver.

PASTE-UP METHODS

To execute a proper paste-up, the consistency of the rubber cement is very important. Four parts cement to one part benzine or thinner will give proper results. The cement should be thin enough to flow freely from the brush.

There are several methods of pasting up. One way is to apply the rubber cement to the surfaces of both pieces and allow this to dry; then adhere. Another method is to apply the cement to one surface; let it dry; cement the other surface; and, while it is still wet, paste together. The beginner should follow this last method. Yet another method is to apply the cement to one side only and paste up while still wet. This is a quick, but not very permanent paste-up and should be used with discretion.

Excess rubber cement can be rubbed off with your finger or with an eraser, but the most practical method is with the "pickup." This is simply a ball of rubber cement accumulated from around the edges of the cement container. A ready-made pickup is also available.

SLIPSHEET METHOD

Owing to the extreme tackiness of rubber cement, it is sometimes difficult to paste large or flimsy material without their buckling or wrinkling. Therefore, the "slipsheet" method is used.

First, cement both surfaces and allow to dry. Then, cover the area to be mounted upon with a clean tissue paper, leaving about ½" of exposed cement at the top or narrowest end (Fig. 33). Dry cement will not adhere to a noncemented surface. Holding the piece to be mounted at both ends, place it upon the tissue, permitting it to adhere lightly to the ½" exposed area (Fig. 34).

Being certain that the mounted sheet is flat and tacked into proper position, slide the tissue from beneath, gradually smoothing it with your hand outward from the center. Then, cover with a clean sheet of paper and burnish air pockets and creases outward from the center. For burnishing, you can use a flat straightedge, such as a plastic triangle. However, burnishing with a plastic device tends to melt or burn away its edge as a result of heat created by the friction, thus destroying the efficiency of the tool. Therefore, keep on hand a triangle to be used only for this purpose.

For mounting large sheets, two tissues are used, overlapping about ½" at the center. The same procedure is employed, slipping out first one tissue, then the other (Figs. 35 and 36).

Fig. 33 *When you rubber cement with the slipsheet method, the tissue must cover all of the remaining cemented area.*

Fig. 34 *Press the piece firmly at the top when you slide the tissue from below.*

Fig. 35 *Only a slight overlap.*

Fig. 36 *Pull out bottom tissue first.*

REMOVING A MOUNTED SHEET

In order to remove a mounted sheet, use thinner (applied with a thinner dispenser), carefully lifting the surface to be removed while pouring. It is very important that the cemented surfaces be clean and free of dirt particles, or impressions will appear after mounting. Sometimes thinner will stain a surface; however, in most instances the stain will be temporary and will dry out in a short time.

ONE-COAT CEMENT

Since *one-coat* cement has become such a part of the artist's materials, the cement referred to above is now commonly called *two-coat* or *regular* rubber cement. One-coat is a much tackier rubber cement which requires only one application to the back of the unit to be mounted.

Many artists consider one-coat a faster and cleaner way to work, due to the relative freedom of manipulation of the unit and the elimination of excess cement clean-up. After the cement has dried, the art is properly positioned, then simply burnished into place.

If the unit has to be repositioned or lifted, use the corner of a razor blade to pull away one corner of the art and lift it with your tweezers. If the art has been burnished too firmly, apply thinner along the edges to loosen it before lifting. Then reposition and burnish. There is no need to recement the unit. But be careful to avoid tearing the art.

You will find one-coat extremely useful for replacing small units or for correcting misspelled words or punctuation. Using it for pasting up on acetate lessens the chore considerably. You'll also find it most helpful in pasting up dummies and layouts.

There are, however, certain aspects of using one-coat that may be troublesome. Due to its extreme tackiness, you'll find it difficult to slip-sheet large units; it sticks to the slipsheet. Try using the wax paper found in the back of some tracing pads or bond pads.

If you turn over a unit with dried one-coat cement on the back, you'll find it will stick to the surface. This is troublesome, and may occur frequently when you want to cut the art. Using waxed paper between the unit and the board you're cutting on does not really help. Use a piece of clean vinyl as a cutting board, or make your own: remove the back cardboard from a pad and completely cover one side with masking tape, overlapping each strip slightly. This makes an excellent cutting board when you've applied one-coat cement.

One last thing about one-coat cement as a word of caution. Its unusually adhesive qualities can create a mess in your files or on your work table because it sticks to anything it touches. Excess pieces thrown haphazardly around your work area can stick to something important and you may throw it away. Razor blades can get caught up in the sticky waste on your table and you may unwittingly cut yourself when crumpling pieces of paper to be thrown away.

There will be occasions when you'll have to remove cement from the back of a unit for one reason or another. This could be quite a problem inasmuch as the pickup will stick to the cement, making it difficult to pull away without tearing the unit. Try this: coat the unit with *two-coat* cement (directly over the one-coat) and let it dry. Then proceed to remove the cement with your pickup in the regular manner.

SPRAY CAN ADHESIVE

The cement in spray cans is similar to one-coat and used in the same manner. Although exceptionally useful when mounting very large units, the excess spray does drift into the outside surrounding areas of the unit being sprayed. This can be quite messy and, needless to say, destructive. Use it with care, being certain to have a sheet of newspaper or something comparable behind the unit to protect the surrounding areas.

If not used frequently, and if not maintained, the spray button on these cans clog with cement and often break down.

WAXING MACHINE

The waxing machine is also a helpful device. It is simple to use but, as with all materials and equipment, its usefulness depends on your needs. The waxing machine coats the back of the unit with a thin layer of wax and is used in the same manner as one-coat cement.

Cement thinner does not dissolve this wax, a factor which can make it troublesome to lift a unit once it has been adhered into position. Try sliding your razor blade flatly along the edge and under it to remove the unit. Once lifted, it can be replaced without rewaxing. However, a unit that has been removed and replaced too often loses some of its tackiness, at least along the edges. This can give your work a messy look and can cause other problems as well. Almost anything can catch onto a loose edge and tear or remove the unit.

2

Type and Its Preparation

Copy is usually created by the copywriter and presented to the art director in typewritten form. The art director must adapt this information to type according to particular specifications, in order to fit the layout.

Basically mathematical, converting copy into type is not complex in itself, but can be perplexing to the beginner. On the other hand, the *use* of type has many esthetic functions in a design. This text will not deal with that aspect, but with the procedure for having type set.

Before you can control the esthetic use of type, you should know the many characteristics of type as a material. There are basically three methods of setting type: hand, machine, and photocomposition.

HAND SET TYPE

Each character or letter—in capitals, lower case, numerals, punctuations, and symbols—is an engraved form set on a piece of metal called a *slug* (Fig. 37).

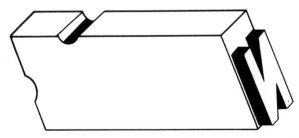

Fig. 37 Each character is engraved on a piece of metal called a slug.

Setting type by hand, the oldest method of all, is done by placing individual slugs into a composing stick, spelling out the copy one character at a time. After the type is set, it is placed into a form, inked with a roller, and printed onto a sheet of paper called a *type proof*. At the completion of proofing, the individual slugs are dissembled and returned to their respective cubicals (cases). This method of typesetting is usually confined to small amounts of type, such as headlines, captions, etc. Setting text by hand could be very expensive and is usually done by machine methods of setting.

MACHINE SET TYPE

There are three kinds of machine equipment used for setting type: Linotype, Monotype, and Ludlow. Although each machine's principle is different, the end result is a complete line of type molded into one long lead slug. Each slug is then grouped to form the text and printed onto proof paper.

PHOTOCOMPOSITION

Photomechanical type (cold type) methods are extremely popular and advantageous in many ways. For example: type set in metal (hot metal type) is a printed image on paper. The size of hot metal type is, however, limited. Few faces are available in sizes larger than 1″ or 1¼″. If you needed a line of type 3″ high, you would have to set it as large as possible, photostat it to 3″, and clean and repair the irregularities. This could be time consuming.

Phototype, on the other hand, is a photographic image which can be printed to almost any size, without irregularities or broken edges. It offers a much sharper, cleaner impression with virtually no restrictions in size.

TYPE TERMINOLOGY

Each letter in the alphabet should be referred to as a *character*. Capitals are called caps or upper case. The small characters are called lower case, consisting of an upper stroke called the *ascender* (as in the letter *b*), and a downward stroke called the *descender* (as in the letter *y*).

The design of a particular alphabet is called *face* or *style*, such as

Helvetica, Caslon, Futura, etc. Type styles can be designed in *roman* (vertical strokes) or in *italics* (slanted strokes). The characters can be designed as simple strokes called *sans serif,* or with crosslines at the end of the main stroke called the *serif.*

Type styles offer a variety of proportions and weights, such as in the type face Futura. Futura looks like this— NORMAL but is also available narrower called **CONDENSED** . Some faces are designed in a series of wider proportions called extended, such as EUROSTILE EUROSTILE EXTENDED , etc.

Many faces are also designed in various weights such as LIGHT, **MEDIUM**, **BOLD.**

The size of type is measured from the top of an ascender to the bottom of the descender in a given alphabet. The scale of measure for type is not calculated in inches or fractions of an inch but in *points.* The inch has been broken down to approximately 72 points, e.g. ½″ would be 36 points, ¼″ would be 18 points. This method affords much more accurate measurements in minute increments.

The length of a line is measured in *picas* (6 picas to 1 inch). The pica is also broken down into points (12 points to 1 pica).

TYPE SPECIFICATION

Typographers offer a catalog of their available type faces called a *type book* or type specimen book. The top of each page lists the name of the type face, and the page consists of a printed alphabet in caps, lower case, and numerals in the various sizes they offer (Fig. 44).

After studying a typical type book, you will notice it is usually broken down into three sections, hand, machine, and photo type. The machine section is for text settings ranging in size from 5 or 6 point to 14 or 18 point as the largest sizes. Larger sizes of the same faces are in the hand section which shows sizes up to 72 points. There are more hand set faces than machine. The photo type section displays both text and headline faces in all sizes.

Fig. 38 illustrates a simple layout consisting of a headline and text. Fig. 39 is the typewritten copy to be converted into type to fit the layout.

SPECIFYING TYPE: STEP ONE

After choosing the type face (Fig. 40), decide upon the size of the face you feel will fit the area indicated in the layout, which will also produce the same look or color to the line. Color, in this instance, means the value

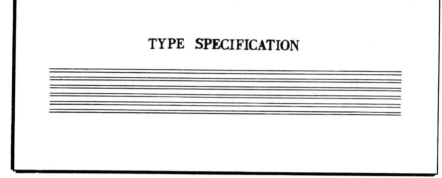

TYPE SPECIFICATION

Fig. 38 The layout: headline and text.

TYPE SPECIFICATION

Type is measured in points and picas.There are
72 points in one inch, 12 points in one pica and
6 picas in one inch. Overall lengths and widths are
usually calculated in picas; whereas the height
of a character and space between lines is measured
in points. When type is set "solid" it means normal
spacing between lines. If a block of copy needs to be
made deeper it can be acomplished by opening the
spaces between lines and inserting a required size
lead slug between each line. This is called "leading"
and is **referre**d to as "1 point lead","2 point lead",etc.

Fig. 39 The typewritten copy to be converted to type in the style indicated by the layout.

BODONI REGULAR

HAND SET

10 POINT

AHIJKLMNOPQRSTUVWXYZABCDEFGHIJKLMNOPQ
abcdefghijklmnopqrstuvwxyz $1234567890

18 POINT

ARSTUVWXYZABCDEFGHIJKLM
abcdefghijklmnopqrstuv $12345678

24 POINT

ANOPQRSTUVWXYZABC
awxyzabcdefghijkl $901234

30 POINT

ADEFG amnopq $5678

36 POINT

AHIJK arstuvw $901

42 POINT

ALMN axyza $23

48 POINT

AOPQ abcd $45

60 POINT

ARS aefg $6

72 POINT

ATU ahij $

Fig. 40 *Bodoni has been chosen as the type face. This is how it might look in a specimen book.*

of gray the line presents. For example, observe the color of this page of text compared with the captions or a page from another textbook.

Suppose you decide on 18 point Bodoni for the headline. Count the characters in the headline (also count each space between words and punctuation mark as a character). The count for this headline is 17 characters.

STEP TWO

Count 17 characters of 18 point Bodoni caps in the type book and measure the length with a pair of dividers or with a ruler. This represents an approximate length the line of type would be if you set it in that face at that size.

STEP THREE

Compare this measurement with the layout. If it is the correct length, you have chosen the correct size. If it is too short, count out the length in the next larger size. If it is too long, count out the length in the next smaller size. Repeat this method for each point size, illustrated on the page, until it measures the required length.

Absolute accuracy is virtually impossible at times. Should your closest calculation be a difference of only ½ character or so too short, you can use that size, instructing the typographer to *lead out* the line to fit the measure needed. *Lead out* means to place a lead slug between each character and/or word to make the line longer. If no lead is needed in a setting, it is referred to as *set solid*.

If your closest calculation is too long by ½ character or so, the typographer cannot help you. You may have to compromise or perhaps set the line and have a photostat made to correct length or use a face in the photo type section.

In the event that you cannot ascertain a compromising size, choose another type face and start over. Once you have made the final decision on face and size, write instructions on the copy sheet (Fig. 41).

STEP FOUR

Count the characters in the typewritten copy. There are several approaches to this, but for the purpose of simplification, we will outline a

Type is measured in points and picas.There are
72 points in one inch, 12 points in one pica and
6 picas in one inch. Overall lengths and widths are
usually calculated in picas; whereas the height
of a character and space between lines is measured
in points. When type is set "solid" it means normal
spacing between lines. If a block of copy needs to be
made deeper it can be acomplished by opening the
spaces between lines and inserting a required size
lead slug between each line. This is called "leading"
and is referred to as "1 point lead","2 point lead",etc.

Fig. 41 *Write instructions for the headline on the copy.*

standard procedure. Once this method is understood, you can develop your own.

The purpose of this count is to determine the approximate total amount of characters in the entire block of copy. For example, if you had a shape measuring 47″ by 11″ and needed to know the square inch area of the space, you would multiply 47″ x 11″ and conclude 517 square inches to be the total area. Using the same formula to determine the total characters in this text, you must first determine the total characters in one line. Because the length of each line is irregular, establish an average length. Draw a vertical line through the copy to approximate an average length (Fig. 42).

Count the characters in one line up to this vertical line (each space between words and punctuation mark is counted as one character). Although the text consists of caps and lower case, all is considered to be lower case in this instance. The count for the first line here would be 47 characters.

Count the number of lines in the text (11) and multiply 47 x 11. Your answer will be 517. Now count the characters to the right of the vertical line. Don't forget the space at the end of each line: 57 characters.

Add 517 and 57. Answer: 574 total characters. You must realize that this

Type is measured in points and picas. There are
72 points in one inch, 12 points in one pica and
6 picas in one inch. Overall lengths and widths are
usually calculated in picas; whereas the height
of a character and space between lines is measured
in points. When type is set "solid" it means normal
spacing between lines. If a block of copy needs to be
made deeper it can be acomplished by opening the
spaces between lines and inserting a required size
lead slug between each line. This is called "leading"
and is referred to as "1 point lead","2 point lead",etc.

Fig. 42 Count the copy by establishing an average line and adding or deducting the characters that do not meet this average.

is an approximation. Each character, capital, lower case, punctuation, and numeral is in a different proportion. An absolute count is impossible. The count is based on the use of the lower case x as an average character. Presumably, if the copy were set using all x's there should be approximately 574. Even this is improbable, which means no one can be positive of any text count. Therefore, you are working with an assumed total.

Nevertheless, the system works quite well when understood, but you must remember that your calculations are flexible. The count could be off as much as 5 or 6 characters in either direction.

STEP FIVE

Measure the width of the text area decided in the layout: 4½" (or 27 picas). At this point, you should choose an appropriate point size if you haven't already. Let's try 8 point.

Note the line of copy above the upper right hand corner of the sample copy (Fig. 43). It reads "characters per inch: lower case 18, caps 12." This is an average character count for you to work with. Not all type books illustrate their count in this fashion. Some have counts broken

BODONI REGULAR with ITALIC and SMALL CAPS
LINOTYPE

6 POINT   Characters per inch: Lower Case 23, Caps 15

THE BEST AND THE MOST DURABLE FASHIONS QUICKLY BECOME DATED W
The best and the most durable fashions quickly become dated whenever styles change. T

THE BEST AND THE MOST DURABLE FASHIONS QUICKLY BECOME DATED W
The best and the most durable fashions quickly become dated whenever styles change. T

ABCDEFGHIJKLMNOPQRSTUVWXYZ $1234567890

8 POINT   Characters per inch: Lower Case 18, Caps 12

THE BEST AND THE MOST DURABLE FASHIONS QUICKLY B
The best and the most durable fashions quickly become dated whenev

THE BEST AND THE MOST DURABLE FASHIONS QUICKLY B
The best and the most durable fashions quickly become dated whenev

ABCDEFGHIJKLMNOPQRSTUVWXYZ $1234567890

9 POINT   Characters per inch: Lower Case 17, Caps 12

THE BEST AND THE MOST DURABLE FASHIONS QUICK
The best and the most durable fashions quickly become dated w

THE BEST AND THE MOST DURABLE FASHIONS QUICK
The best and the most durable fashions quickly become dated w

ABCDEFGHIJKLMNOPQRSTUVWXYZ $1234567890

10 POINT   Characters per inch: Lower Case 15.5, Caps 10

THE BEST AND THE MOST DURABLE FASHIONS QU
The best and the most durable fashions quickly become da

THE BEST AND THE MOST DURABLE FASHIONS QU
The best and the most durable fashions quickly become da

ABCDEFGHIJKLMNOPQRSTUVWXYZ $1234567890

11 POINT   Characters per inch: Lower Case 14.5, Caps 9

THE BEST AND THE MOST DURABLE FASHIONS
The best and the most durable fashions quickly become

THE BEST AND THE MOST DURABLE FASHIONS
The best and the most durable fashions quickly become

ABCDEFGHIJKLMNOPQRSTUVWXYZ $1234567890

12 POINT   Characters per inch: Lower Case 14, Caps 9

THE BEST AND THE MOST DURABLE FASHIO
The best and the most durable fashions quickly beco

THE BEST AND THE MOST DURABLE FASHIO
The best and the most durable fashions quickly beco

ABCDEFGHIJKLMNOPQRSTUVWXYZ $1234567890

14 POINT   Characters per inch: Lower Case 12.5, Caps 8

THE BEST AND THE MOST DURABLE FA
The best and the most durable fashions quickly

THE BEST AND THE MOST DURABLE FA
The best and the most durable fashions quickly

ABCDEFGHIJKLMNOPQRSTUVWXYZ $1234567890

Fig. 43 Note the character count that is given with the type face.

down in picas in the front or back of the book under various type face listings; some have pull-out sheets with counts for each face and size, etc. There are several ways in which typographers offer these calculations.

You are working with lower case and there are 18 characters to 1 inch. The layout is 4½" wide. Multiply 4.5 x 18. The answer, 81, indicates that there will be that many characters in 1 line if set in 8 point Bodoni.

STEP SIX

If 81 characters will be used to fill 1 line, the remaining question is, "how many lines of copy will 574 characters occupy?" Divide 81 into 574. Answer: 7 lines with 6 characters left over. The 7 lines mean 7 complete lines. The 6 extra characters should be disregarded. Therefore, the type will occupy 7 lines of depth.

STEP SEVEN

You know how *wide* the copy will be because you have already determined that, but now you need to know how *deep* it will be.

If your calculations indicate 7 lines of depth and you are using 8 point (height) type, multiply 8 point x 7 lines. Answer: 56 points. The text will be 56 points or approximately 4½ picas deep; which can be found on your pica rule in picas or points.

There are several "scales" available which are an enormous aid in spacing type. For example, see Fig. 44. Here is how it is used. After determining the amount of lines (Step six), you place the scale over the layout, align the top mark in the 8 point slot with the top of the text area and count down 7 lines; that is, how deep 7 lines of 8 point type will be. (Fig. 45) Simple?

Fig. 44 This is a type scale.

Fig. 45 *Lay the type scale down on the layout.*

So much for the mathematics of type specification. Needless to say, you will have to review these steps several times before you get the feel of it. Now let's carry the subject just a bit further. Suppose the 7 lines of depth is *not quite deep enough* to fill the area as in the layout. You have one of several decisions to make. Repeat the procedure, using a larger size, say 10 point, or try a different type face in the same size, or change the layout, or perhaps have the typographer open the space between each line to fit the depth (leading).

Leading between lines is usually done in points. For example 2 points of lead between each line would be a possible leading. If 2 point leading is your decision, when using the scale you would not read the 8 point slot, but the 10 point slot (8 point + 2 point lead), down to 7. This gives approximately 2 points of lead between each line.

If you discover 7 lines of 8 point type to be *too deep* for the layout, you *cannot take space out*, because these calculations are based on setting the type *solid* (butting each line of metal), so that they cannot be placed any closer. You can possibly try a smaller size, another type face, or you can change the layout.

The block of copy you worked with in this exercise is to be set *flush left* and *flush right*; i.e. the length of each line is the same. If your layout looked like Fig. 46, it would be called *flush left—rag* (ragged) *right*. In Fig. 47 it would be called *flush right—rag left*. Fig. 48 is *rag left* and *right*. Fig. 49 shows *centered lines*.

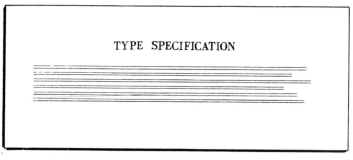

Fig. 46 Flush left, ragged right.

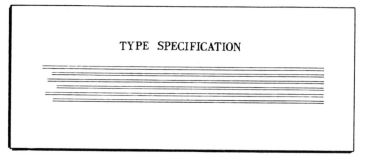

Fig. 47 Flush right, ragged left.

Fig. 48 Ragged left and right.

Fig. 49 Centered lines.

At the conclusion of your calculations, you must legibly write out the instructions to the typographer. I cannot overemphasize the importance of legibility and neatness in writing your specifications. Avoid using *ink* for this; you may have to make changes. Your specs for this job, if set solid, would look like Fig. 50.

TYPE SPECIFICATION

Type is measured in points and picas. There are 72 points in one inch, 12 points in one pica and 6 picas in one inch. Overall lengths and widths are usually calculated in picas; whereas the height of a character and space between lines is measured in points. When type is set "solid" it means normal spacing between lines. If a block of copy needs to be made deeper it can be accomplished by opening the spaces between lines and inserting a required size lead slug between each line. This is called "leading" and is referred to as "1 point lead", "2 point lead", etc.

Fig. 50 Type set solid.

If set with 2 point lead: 8/10 point Bodoni 27 picas wide caps and lower case, flush left and right

TYPE SPECIFICATION

Type is measured in points and picas. There are 72 points in one inch, 12 points in one pica and 6 picas in one inch. Overall lengths and widths are usually calculated in picas; whereas the height of a character and space between lines is measured in points. When type is set "solid" it means normal spacing between lines. If a block of copy needs to be made deeper it can be accomplished by opening the spaces between lines and inserting a required size lead slug between each line. This is called "leading" and is referred to as "1 point lead", "2 point lead", etc.

Fig. 51 Type set with 2 point lead.

HANDLING TYPE PROOFS

The type proof should be handled with great care. When freshly printed, it will smear at the slightest touch. Therefore, it should be "fixed" before using. Liquid sprays or powder are the most effective fixatives. To use a spray, simply follow the directions on the can. However, be careful not to apply it too heavily, or it may blur the type and become very tacky. Powdering type proofs should be done with care, for too much powder may gray the ink. Just sprinkle it onto the proof and spread it lightly with cotton.

When you have mounted the proof with rubber cement, wipe the surface gently with clean cotton. Examine the type proof thoroughly for broken or marred letters, which often appear. It is your job to repair the type with poster paint or India ink. A template pen or fine crowquill may be useful for this.

Along with the type proof a "glassine," or "onionskin," proof is printed. An almost transparent paper, it is especially useful in checking the type against the layout for proper size and position. This proof should also be fixed.

Once the proof has been fixed, cement the back and allow it to dry. Place the proof back down onto a clean cardboard. (The back of a pad is useful here.) Then, with a razor blade, either cut out all the type to be used, or cut as you need it. Scissors also may be used.

DESIGNING WITH PHOTOCOMPOSITION

Because photocomposition can be enlarged to any size without irregularities or broken edges, it is very handy for the designer. In addition to this, photocomposition offers unlimited possibilities in design and arrangement of type. The characters can be tilted, curved, squashed, extended, reduced, and enlarged. They can be overlapped, made in perspective, and distorted. You will find phototype extremely useful in designing book jackets, album covers, brochures, presentations, 35MM slides, or anything requiring large type or unusual arrangements of type. Photocomposition also offers solutions for difficult shapes and sizes in body copy (text). There is no restriction in point size. For example, hot metal offers very specific sizes for each face, 6, 8, 9, 10, 11 point, etc. But with phototype, you can set 9½ point, 11¾ point or whichever size is required. It is set to fit.

When ordering phototype, supply the typographer with a fairly accurate layout, proper typewritten copy, and the type face desired and the approximate point size. It will all be set in position to proper size and arrangement. Simple, from the art director's point of view, but not inexpensive.

POSITIONING TYPE

Various procedures for aligning type may be employed. One method is to line up the bottom of the type with a T-square, then with a blue pencil to lightly draw a line at either extreme of the type, both horizontally and vertically, signifying a corner. Corresponding lines should be drawn on the board (mechanical) in the desired position. Apply cement to the board and allow it to dry or, while it is still wet, position the type, matching the lines on the proof with those on the mechanical (Fig. 52). Tweezers or razor blades are used in manipulating type. With the corner of a razor blade or with tweezers "tack" the type down into position. Then, check for squareness with a T-square.

For faster results, just draw a horizontal and a vertical line on the board, indicating one corner where your type is to be positioned, and line up your type directly on the board with a T-square and triangle, adjusting with forefinger and thumb, tweezers, or any suitable device for manipulation (Fig. 53).

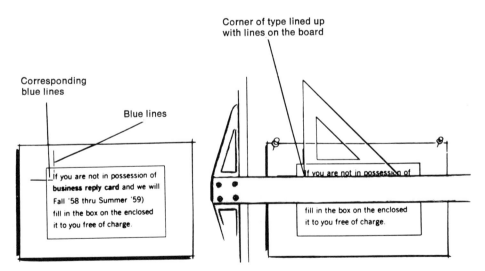

Corner of type lined up with lines on the board

Corresponding blue lines

Blue lines

If you are not in possession of
business reply card and we will
Fall '58 thru Summer '59)
fill in the box on the enclosed
it to you free of charge.

If you are not in possession of

fill in the box on the enclosed
it to you free of charge.

Fig. 52 The blue lines are aligned, but type is not square.

Fig. 53 Be certain that blue lines are still aligned.

A quicker way is to place the type visually in the approximate position and, using your dividers to calculate the actual position, adjust the type. For the beginner, this last method may be too tricky. At the start, it would be best to use one of the other methods. You will gradually develop your own system.

If you should use the dry cement method of pasting large areas of type, slipsheets placed under the type proof will be very convenient. If, while mounting type, the cement should be too tacky, preventing freedom of manipulation, you may apply thinner to dissolve the cement, thus permitting easier shifting of type. If you do this, wait until the cement has dried beneath the proof before pressing it firmly into position, or it may slide out of square. Wet cement may also squeeze out and over the type, causing it to smear.

Probably the best approach for positioning type is to use the glassine. Simply place the glassine type proof (see page 36) over the layout, lining up the copy properly. Mark off the corners of the ad, or make any other suitable key marks for registration. Then position the glassine in the identical position, using the corresponding registration marks on the mechanical. Tape the glassine down at the top. Lift the glassine with one hand and slide the type proof beneath it with the other. After matching the type proof with the glassine, lift the glassine and adjust the type proof for squareness and accuracy of position with a T-square. Then press firmly.

Where a glassine cannot be used (such as with art, photos, shapes, etc.), the layout, if on transparent (tracing or visual bond) paper, may be taped into position onto the mechanical. Follow the same procedure as in the use of the glassine. Simply lift the layout, place the piece to be mounted beneath it, and line it up with the indication on the layout. If the layout is not on transparent paper, you may make a fairly accurate tracing of the over-all size of each element in the layout and follow the same procedure.

Centering type or any element is not always done mechanically for the simple reason that a line of type (although perfectly centered within an area) may appear to be off-center. This is rectified by raising the line slightly above-center until it is optically centered. As long as the element *looks* centered, according to your judgment, it should be sufficient, except in cases when an element must be mechanically centered because of production or technical reasons. However, in most jobs, this optical centering should be sufficient.

TRANSFER TYPE

Transfer or rub-off sheets are especially useful in preparing dummies, layouts, presentations and, if used with care, can be used for reproduction. The type character or numeral is printed on a wax backed, thin acetate film. When the type is placed, waxed side down, onto a surface, burnished and lifted, the character is transferred from the sheet to the surface. By using the printed guide lines with each character, several can be aligned to produce a word or words. They are available in several sizes and faces in black or color. Prestype type sheets are also useful. There the type is not transferred, but is simply burnished in position and then cut out.

RE-SPACING TYPE

After it is set, type does not always fit the space indicated in the layout. Because of this, some compensation must be made. Perhaps a photostat (which will be explained later) of the type reduced or enlarged will solve the problem. But more than likely if you "open up" or "close up" the space between the lines ("line-spacing"), it will fit. In addition to adjusting the space between the lines, you may have to open or close up the space between the words ("word-spacing") or between the letters ("letter-spacing").

The following system may be used in line-spacing type to fit another size or shape. First, cement the proof into the approximate position. Then, with a razor blade and a steel T-square, cut between each line (Fig. 54). Wet this down with thinner and slide each line (with the corner of razor blade or tweezers) away from the others, opening the spaces between them until the desired size has been reached (Fig. 55). Be certain that the space between each line is the same. Use your dividers as a guide.

To close up the space, make two cuts between each line, wet down the area with thinner, and pull out the space. Note: thinner will not affect the type. Then push each line closer (Figs. 56, 57, and 58).

If word-spacing or letter-spacing is required, use the same method as in line-spacing. The only difference is that the cut marks are made between the letters or words, and you either push them together or pull them apart, being certain that they are kept "square" with your T-square and triangle (Figs. 59 and 60).

Cutting directly on the mechanical is sometimes frowned upon by the

> If you are not in possession of
> **business reply card** and we will
> Fall '58 thru Summe
> fill in the box o
> it to you free of

> If you are not in possession of
> **business reply card** and we will
> Fall '58 thru Summer '59)
> fill in the box on the enclosed
> it to you free of charge.

Fig. 54 When re-spacing type, cut between each line with a fresh blade.

Fig. 55 With tweezers, pull away each line until you reach the spacing you desire.

> Selector are your key
> 3 items are also available
> service plus your normal stock
> In-Stock servic
> to ever increasi

> Selector are your key
> 3 items are also available
> service plus your normal stock
> In-Stock service. The In-Stock
> to ever increasing

Fig. 56 To close up space between lines, make two cuts between each line.

Fig. 57 Pull out spaces.

> Selector are your key
> 3 items are also available
> service plus your normal stock
> In-Stock service. The In-Stock
> to ever increasing

Fig. 58 Push lines together.

Fig. 59 *To letter-space, cut apart each letter freehand.*

Fig. 60 *Pull apart the letters, without letting the tweezers touch the type.*

art director. It does leave unsightly cut marks on the mechanical if done carelessly or if an element must be moved after cutting. Nevertheless, it is a very accurate and convenient method.

Of course, there are other ways to achieve the same results. After having cemented the back of the type proof, you might cut each line separately on a cutting board and place each one individually on the mechanical, adjusting them until the required size is attained.

Some artists do their re-spacing on a separate piece of two-ply Strathmore, then cut the new arrangement out as a unit and place it in position on the mechanical. This method avoids cut marks on the mechanical and, in the event that the type has to be shifted or repositioned, this can be done without having to re-space the type again.

CURVING TYPE

Although type can be curved photomechanically, it is possible that time and budget may not permit this approach, in which case you must do this in your mechanical. No matter where you work, you will inevitably have to curve type at one time or another. There are two excellent methods of doing this.

Fig. 61 shows a rough layout of a line of curved type. Fig. 62 is the type as it is printed (proof). Place a sheet of tracing paper over the layout and make a very accurate pencil line of the desired curve, either along the bottom or top edge of the type. Use a French curve and a 6H pencil.

Indicate the beginning and end of the line of type. Tape this tracing over a sheet of two ply Strathmore (Fig. 63). Lift the tissue back. Coat the paper with rubber cement and allow it to dry. Cement the back of the type proof and allow it to dry.

At this stage, you can curve your type in one of two methods. The first one is as follows. Place the cemented type face up onto a clean piece of chip board (the back of a pad), then cut away the excess paper around it to facilitate handling. Do not cut closer than $\frac{1}{16}''$ or so. Carefully cut around each character with a razor blade (or one character at a time as needed) as shown in Fig. 64.

Bring the tissue back over the cemented paper. Holding it at the bottom with your left hand, raise it slightly from the surface. Lift the first character from the type proof with your tweezers and position it under the tracing. Very carefully, line up the character with the pencil indication on the tissue. Anchor it into position by pressing the corner of the piece with your tweezers. When manipulating in this manner, be careful not to mar the type.

Repeat the same procedure with the last character (Fig. 65). You now have the limits set for the length of the line. Work between them. Now, *roughly*, position each character in the same manner, controlling the space between them optically (Fig. 66). Do not press them down at this stage. It is too soon to set them permanently.

If you work carefully and simply, resting each letter on the paper, it will be easier to manipulate them. Once you have pressed it, the cement will grip, making it difficult to move the pieces. This takes a bit of practice, but if your cement is mixed to the proper consistency, you can actually lift and reposition the pieces without having to wet them down with thinner, in the beginning at least.

After you have roughly positioned all the pieces beneath the tissue, lift the tissue back and continue manipulating further. If pieces become difficult to move, wet them with thinner. *Do not flood the paper.* Just a slight squirt of thinner will be sufficient. Some artists apply thinner with a small brush or an eye dropper.

Now bring the tissue down in place and check the type for proper curve. Lift the tissue and adjust the type further if needed. Once again, bring the tissue down over the assembly, and check it. Lift the tissue and adjust; bring the tissue down and check; lift the tissue and adjust. Repeat this until you have all the characters lined up properly and readably spaced.

Do not burnish into position while the cement is wet or the pieces will shift. Lift the tissue and allow the cement to dry around and beneath the pieces. When dry, place a piece of tissue over the assembly and burnish into position, firmly.

curving type

Fig. 61 A rough layout of a line of curved type.

curving type

Fig. 62 The type has been set in a straight line.

Fig. 63 The tracing paper—indicating the desired curve—is taped over a board.

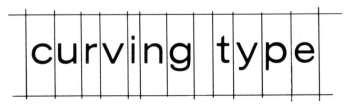

Fig. 64 Cut above, below, and between each printed letter.

Fig. 65 *Position first and last character, using the tissue overlay as a guide.*

Fig. 66 *Position each letter roughly.*

Fig. 67 After cleaning around the type, the end result should look like this.

Fig. 68A The second method of curving type: cut between each letter from the top to just below the bottom edge.

Fig. 68B Or you can cut from below to nearly the top edge, if you are curving type in the opposite direction.

Fig. 69 The end result of the second method of curving type. Type is fanned out to the curve.

Make a final check with the tissue to be certain that the pieces did not shift. The cut marks around the characters often deceive your judgment in spacing. If you look at it through your tracing paper (pulled slightly away from the surface), these lines will become diffused, permitting a better impression of the placement of the characters.

Clean up the excess cement from around the pieces. This is where your nerves are put to the test. After spending twenty minutes manipulating these pieces into position, one or two may pull away while you pick up the rubber cement. This is especially true when working with small characters. Try pressing the flat end of your tweezers on each piece as you clean around it. This will help. If a piece repeatedly comes up, you can cement it in position again or use a white water soluble glue instead of cement. You can also try a dab of white poster paint as a glue.

In many instances, a piece will overlap an adjoining piece after it has been curved. You will obviously have to cut it away with a razor blade. However, with small pieces, *do not use a cutting motion,* i.e., do not *pull* the blade across the piece. This may tear it or pull it out of position. Actually, it is best to position the blade where you want to cut and then *press,* rather than pull. The excess will snap away. The end result should look like Fig. 67.

The second method for curving type is as follows. Follow the same preliminary procedures as before to the point of cutting out each character. Now, rather than cut out each character, you can cut between each from the top to just below the bottom edge (Fig. 68A). Should the curve bend in the opposite direction, cut from the bottom to the top edge of each character (Fig. 68B).

Position the entire line beneath the tissue, aligning it with the curve. Then, lightly, wet the unit with thinner and bend the line according to the indication of the required curve. Each character will fan out. This takes a fair amount of manipulation and is a rather direct approach. However, the line has a tendency to buckle. Should it be too short for the full length of the curve, you will have to cut it apart anyway. The end result should look like Fig. 69.

Wet cement invariably transfers to the underside of the tracing during the manipulation. Keep rubbing it away from the tissue or it may stick to the characters and pull them away when you lift the tissue. Of course, if you are using "one coat" cement the entire procedure is less messy and perhaps faster. However, the use of either type of cement is a matter of personal choice.

3

Components of
the Mechanical

A printed advertisement cannot be produced without some sort of printing plate. The printing plate cannot be made without some sort of original composite of the elements involved. The mechanical is this original makeup, consisting of all the components in their respective positions precisely as they are to appear on the printed page. The printing plate is made directly from this mechanical (Figs. 70 and 71).

In order to prepare a mechanical properly, its "language" must be learned. Particular rules are observed to make the mechanical's requirements visually understandable to the cameraman, such as the use of crop marks, bleed, screen indications, etc. In this chapter, some of the basic components on the mechanical—particularly the handling of art work—will be discussed.

Even though the rules given here are a *must* in all mechanicals, the methods of execution may vary according to the agency or the platemaker with whom you will be working. This will be discussed more thoroughly later on.

PHOTOSTATS

One of the most serviceable facilities in assembling a paste-up or mechanical is the photostat. The basic difference between a photostat and a photograph is that the stat negative is opaque paper and the photo negative is transparent film. A photostat is much less expensive than a regular photograph, and both the negative and positive can be very useful. For instance, if the layout calls for white type on a black back-

LIVE A LITTLE

EUROPE·AFRICA AND THE MIDDLE EAST

as low as

$28.30 per day

sknaht: dehcnic ti dah eh, ylluterger laa ta ton snialpxe eh sa, esuaceb Elay ta Hcne am eh, tcaf ni taht ddn retsgunoy a sa Eporue ni emit hcum tneps Ycrad wnok oh wef yrev eht ot gniffab erom eht lla. Yldrah. Msilaicnvorp nretesw nrob buts fo elm rentre Naeporue a, ta deiks elnol tel, detisiv neve reven sa ah dna, anacs wnos lan eht no nem laitneulfni tsom eht fo eno si eh ereh. Srebmun etisoppo dna seugealloc si

Fig. 70 All units are pasted up in this mechanical for an advertisement.

LIVE A LITTLE

EUROPE·AFRICA AND THE MIDDLE EAST

as low as $28.30 per day

sknaht: dehcnic ti dah eh, ylluterger laa ta ton snialpxe eh sa, esuaceb Elay ta Hcne am eh, tcaf ni taht ddn retsgunoy a sa Eporue ni emit hcum tneps Ycrad wnok oh wef yrev eht ot gniffab erom eht lla. Yldrah. Msilaicnvorp nretesw nrob buts fo elm rentre Naeporue a, ta deiks elnol tel, detisiv neve reven sa ah dna, anacs wnos lan eht no nem laitneulfni tsom eht fo eno si eh ereh. Srebmun etisoppo dna seugealloc si

Fig. 71 No cut marks show in the printed page.

ground (reversed copy), you will obtain the proper results by ordering a negative stat of the original black type (Figs. 72 and 73).

Although there are various types of stat paper available, generally you will be concerned with two—the matte and the glossy. Matte stats hold, with limited accuracy, various gradations of tone values (similar to the photograph), while the glossy is confined to black and white with no intermediate values. (See chapter on photoengraving.)

The stat has a variety of uses in paste-ups and mechanicals. For example, in assembling a dummy or layout where artwork or photos are required, a stat is used instead in order to preserve the actual art or photo. In preparing a mechanical, the same procedure is followed, especially when the art is not actual reproduction size. A stat of the art, reduced or enlarged to required size and placed in position on the mechanical, acts as a visual guide for size and position for the cameraman and platemaker to follow. It also shows the mechanical man whether or not the art will fit into its proper position or if it meets the requirements of the layout.

Because the matte stat is not a true representation of the art in its proper tonal values, it is used just for the purpose of showing size and position of the art in the mechanical and under very few circumstances for reproduction.

The glossy stat, on the other hand, may be used for reproduction. Because of its sharpness of black and white areas, it is very often used as a means of reducing or enlarging lettering, type, line drawings, etc., and can be properly positioned in the mechanical. However, a glossy stat of tone art, such as a photo or wash drawing, will break up and appear blotchy. Values of gray of less than fifty percent intensity will tend to bleach out, while those over fifty percent will tend to fill in, resulting in a very poor representation of the original art. Therefore, the art must have no values of gray if it is to produce a good, clean black and white line glossy photostat to be used for reproduction.

When a negative stat is cemented onto a black background, be certain to blacken the edges around the stat after cutting it out (see page 113). This will prevent paste-up and cut marks from appearing on the cameraman's negatives and will eliminate unnecessary work for the film stripper (Fig. 74).

Another advantage of the photostat is that, if necessary, a reverse position print of the art can be made. This is called "flopping" the art. It comes in handy if your art is facing one way and the layout calls for it to face the other way (Figs. 75 and 76).

come in and

Fig. 72 *A positive stat shows black type on white background.*

come in and

Fig. 73 *A negative stat shows white type on black background.*

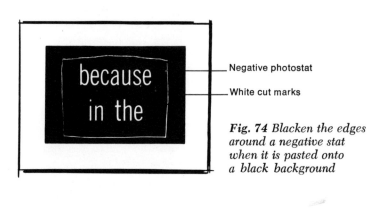

because in the

Negative photostat

White cut marks

Fig. 74 *Blacken the edges around a negative stat when it is pasted onto a black background*

Fig. 75 *Here is the original art.*

Fig. 76 *The original art has been flopped (not reversed) in the stat.*

HOW TO ORDER PHOTOSTATS

Figs. 77 to 82 show several procedures employed in ordering stats. The method you choose is entirely up to the requirements of the original copy, the organization you work for or the stat house being used.

For the sake of economy and time, it is advisable, when more than one piece is to be statted in the same proportion (focus), to assemble ("gang up") as many as possible on one board and have it statted as a unit. Subsequently, one print will contain all units for the cost of one.

When you want a particular portion of the original blown up (whether you use a photostat or photograph), be certain to indicate this on your

1 s/s glossy (or matte) neg: (or pos.)

Fig. 77 *Here is how you indicate the art for a same size (s/s) photostat.*

|← 11" BM (between marks) →|
1 glossy (or matte) neg. (and/or pos.)

Fig. 78 *For a reduction or enlargement, indicate with two marks the extremes needed. Connect these marks with arrows and write instuctions. This may be done on the back of the original copy, on a tissue taped over it, or in the margin.*

|← 4" BM →|
This is pos., 1 glossy (or matte) neg.

Fig. 79 *Frequently, the original copy seems to be a negative when actually it is a positive (or vice-versa). In order to prevent confusion, you might indicate that the original art is negative or positive.*

|← 4" BM →|
1 glossy (or matte) 1st (and/or 2nd) print

Fig. 80 *Another solution to this problem is to refer to the negative or positive as a first or second print. If you want the opposite impression of the original copy, ask for a first print. When the same impression is needed, ask for a second print.*

1 glossy neg. (your measure of the orig. copy)↑ (enlarged to) 17"
1 glossy neg. 4" (reduced to) ↓ 2"

Fig. 81 *The distance between the marks you indicate on the copy (Fig. 78) is measured at the stat house, and a percentage for the reduction or enlargement is worked out. To avoid error, you might write the measurements yourself.*

For same size

1 glossy 1st print s/s

For reduction

1 glossy 1st print (and/or 2nd print) 4" ↓ 2"

For enlargement

1 glossy 1st print 4" ↑ 13"

Fig. 82 *By giving full instructions, according to Figs. 80 and 81, you will avoid the possibility of error.*

Fig. 83 *Here is the original art properly marked for a blow-up. Be specific.*

Fig. 84 *Here is the art blown-up (11" x 14").*

Fig. 85 *If the area had not been properly marked, the blow-up would have looked like this (18" x 24").*

order, on a tissue over the art, or on the back of the art. Simply circle or box in the area and write "Take in just this area." Otherwise, the cameraman will have no way of knowing you need only a particular area and he will naturally assume he is to take in the entire artwork. For example, Fig. 83 shows the art properly marked for the blow-up in Fig. 84. If the area desired had *not* been marked properly, the stat might have come back looking like Fig. 85. This is a common error and can be avoided with a little forethought. One is waste enough, but several at one time can be very exasperating.

BLEACHING STATS

You will find a bleaching kit very helpful in working with stats or photos in both finished art and for preparing dummies or presentations. For example, you can erase a line of type or area without having to blacken the negative or reshoot it. It is good for general cleanup if you prefer not to use white paint.

GHOSTED STATS

For some subjects, it may be best to order a grayed-down stat (ghosted) to about a 50% value, just enough to see the object in detail and not too dark to interfere with the black inking. This method is particularly useful in preparing line drawings of industrial subjects. If you have a photograph of the subject, shoot a stat of it to a comfortable drawing size and proceed as just described.

In preparing dummies, presentations of layouts that may call for stats of type, for example, to be painted over in another color, it would be much easier if you ordered the stats "ghosted." The paint will cover it with less trouble and will look much neater.

PERSPECTIVE STATS

The perspective stat is a helpful service. For difficult line drawings of items or products that have labels or involved shapes, you can send the actual item to the stat house and have it statted in the perspective you need. You can then trace or draw from the stat. If there is a label on the item and you want it reproduced, you can cut it out of the stat and paste it onto your drawing. Be certain it is sharp black and white. If it is not, touch it up. Type and art can also be shot in perspective.

When ordering a perspective shot, you *must* send along a sketch of the over-all shape in the perspective you want. Sketch directly from the object; do not attempt to draw it from memory if you expect any degree of accuracy. Remember, the stat may not match the sketch perfectly, because statting in perspective is a difficult thing to accomplish and requires skill on the part of the cameraman. If you are going to use it only as a guide in preparing your finished art, you can make adjustments later. If possible, lucy the item (in outline) to the size and perspective you want. This will be much more accurate and closer to what the stat camera will see.

A lucy, incidentally, is a camera device for projecting an enlargement or reduction of artwork or anything that can be placed flat in the machine. It projects the subject onto paper, or through tracing paper, enabling you to visualize effectively the artwork in its new dimension. The lucy is useful for scaling photos, art, type, layouts, and is an enormous help to illustrators and designers.

Needless to say, photostats have many uses. If ever you are confronted with an unusual problem, there is a chance that it can be solved photostatically. The best thing to do is to call your stat man and present him with your problem. He may be able to solve it, or at least he may offer a constructive suggestion.

DRAWING PERSPECTIVE

In illustrations (particularly industrial subjects) where an involved perspective calls for vanishing points beyond the capacity of your drawing table, you might try making your initial drawing a smaller, more convenient size, have it photostatted up to finished size, and trace it off. Or you can use your light box to trace it on the *back* of the stat (making revisions); then place the stat face up in position on the illustration board and rub it down, transferring the pencil drawing from the back of the stat to the illustration board. If you are working on a thin enough Strathmore, you will be able to trace the stat directly with the light box.

MARKING PHOTOGRAPHS

Photographs are frequently used in advertising. They are costly; therefore, proper handling is essential.

Never write on the surface or on the back of the photo with a hard pencil; the markings will crease the emulsion of the photo and perhaps mar it. If marking or writing is unavoidable, use a grease crayon on the front, the back, or on a tissue taped over the photo. The grease crayon can be removed from the emulsion side with thinner and cotton. *Caution: it may stain.*

If you use felt tip pens for marking photos, do so with discretion. The ink from felt tip pens may be removed with thinner or perhaps with some soapy water or cotton, but be careful not to destroy the emulsion of the photo.

MOUNTING PHOTOS WITH A DRY MOUNT PRESS

A dry mount press (Fig. 86), also referred to as a *hot mount,* is permanent and probably the best method of mounting photos. The press itself consists of an electrically heated metal plate that is pressed against the photo which has been placed over the mounting board. A sheet of "dry mount tissue"—a thin sheet, resembling heavy wax paper—is placed between the back of the photo and the mounting board (Fig. 87). The tissue, having a dry adhesive on both sides, is heated by the electric plate, softening the adhesive. While the hot plate is forced against the mounting surface, the heat forces the glue into the fiber of the back of the photo and the surface of the mounting board. When the heated plate is removed, the glue hardens, fusing the photo to the board. Once mounted, the photo cannot be removed.

Fig. 86 Dry mount press.

Fig. 87 The tissue, placed between the back of the photo and the mounting board—must be trimmed flush with the edges of the photo.

MOUNTING PHOTOS WITHOUT A PRESS

For mounting a photograph securely, when a dry mount press is not available, use double coats of cement on both surfaces and slipsheet them. Coating both surfaces with "one coat" cement will offer a much more permanent mounting. But before mounting, be certain to check the back of the photo for names, key numbers, identification, etc. This information should be transferred to the back of the board upon which the photo is to be mounted. *Caution:* you will often find photos have slips of paper containing relative data pasted on the back. This paper should be removed carefully and cemented onto the back of the board after mounting. If it is not removed, its impression will show up on the face of the photo.

When mounting a photograph, leave a wide margin around the photo (2″ or more) for written production instructions and for protection of the edges. Mount onto a smooth, heavy stock—never use pebbled matboard. After mounting, place a sheet of bond paper over the photo and burnish the photo flat with a straightedge.

A layout will frequently call for photos to be used smaller or larger than the original. In such cases, a photostat is made, bringing it down or up to the required size. This stat is placed in position on the mechanical and crossed out with a red pencil. The stat serves only as a guide for size and position. The original is mounted separately and sent along with the mechanical to the cameraman. The cameraman, upon shooting his negatives, will make a separate negative directly from the original photo (in the focus indicated by the stat) and combine ("strip in") the negatives accordingly.

SILHOUETTING

Quite often a layout will require a silhouetted photo in which the edges of the image are silhouetted. It is your job to white out the areas not needed in the photo. To begin with, the surface of the photo is often greasy, making it extremely difficult for paint to adhere. Several methods can be employed to overcome this. One of them is the use of "pounce," a powdery substance which can be sprinkled and rubbed over the emulsion and cleaned away with a dry tissue or handkerchief. This gives a slight "tooth" to the emulsion. Another method of rendering a more sympathetic surface to the photo is the use of "non-crawl," which is mixed with the paint, giving it an adhesive quality. Saliva or thinner, rubbed

Fig. 88 To silhouette, first outline with a heavy line of white paint around the desired area.

Fig. 89 Keeping the coverage uniform, apply a border of white paint approximately ½".

Tape

Edge of mask

Silhouetted edge

Fig. 90 *Place a mask onto the photo in such a position that it overlaps the white without touching the silhouetted edge.*

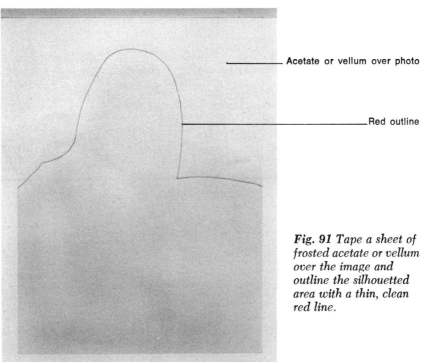

Acetate or vellum over photo

Red outline

Fig. 91 *Tape a sheet of frosted acetate or vellum over the image and outline the silhouetted area with a thin, clean red line.*

on with cotton, often will serve the purpose. The most desirable method depends upon the individual and his experience.

Using white paint and a good brush, start to silhouette by meticulously outlining the entire shape with a line about the weight of a heavy pencil line (Fig. 88). Then, paint a border of white approximately ½″ wide along this line (Fig. 89). The thin outline will act as a wall along the edge, which will enable you to flow the paint along its edge.

It is better to build up the paint with thin coats rather than to attempt complete coverage with a single thick layer. If too thick, the paint may flake and crack off.

At the completion of the silhouetting (and when the paint has thoroughly dried), place a sheet of medium weight bond over the entire photo. Lightly trace a line along the center of the white border. Then, place the bond onto a piece of cardboard and cut out the outlined area. Place this "mask" onto the photo in such a position as to overlap the white, but not to touch the silhouetted edge. This will automatically white out the remaining unwanted areas, without disturbing the silhouetted edge (Fig. 90). Then cut the top edge of the mask about ½″ shorter than the board and secure this with a length of tape across the top. Turn the board over and trim off any excess paper. Write any needed information along the edge of the mask or on a tissue taped over it, being certain not to write over an area of the photo.

In the event that the silhouetted photo in its entirety is needed later, the silhouetted area may be washed off with cotton and water. *Caution:* the emulsion may bubble, peel, or tear if saturated or rubbed too hard. Never silhouette a photo before mounting it firmly onto a heavy stock. If silhouetting is done before mounting, the photo will buckle and the paint will crack or flake off, making it difficult to mount without damaging the photo.

If there is only one photo available and the layout indicates that the photo is to appear in one area in its entirety and silhouetted in another, the photo may be prepared in the following manner.

Mount the photo and key it to correspond with the mechanical. Then tape a sheet of frosted acetate or vellum over it and outline the silhouetted area with a thin red line (Fig. 91). This will enable the cameraman to shoot the complete coverage of the photo and use the red outline as a guide in silhouetting (opaquing) his *negative* for the second shot.

4

Applied Methods of the Mechanical Makeup

There are two types of art: *line* and *continuous tone.* Line art, such as black and white line drawings, type, etc., contains no gray; that is, no intermediate values of black and white (Fig. 92).

Continuous tone art consists of a range of values from white through black: photo, wash drawing, oil painting, etc. (Fig. 93).

PHOTOENGRAVING FOR LETTERPRESS PRINTING

In order to reproduce the respective effects of line and continuous tone art, a metal image (engraving) must be made of the art. This is achieved through a process called photoengraving. Essentially, photoengraving is a method of recreating photographically line and/or continuous tone art on a metal printing plate. The following is a simplification of the complex method employed to make such plates. For our purpose, we will concentrate on understanding the *principle* and *essence* of this process rather than becoming involved too deeply in the mechanics. For further information see the list of reference books at the end of this volume.

LINE ART

First, a photographic negative is made of the art. Then, a sheet of polished zinc, copper, or magnesium metal, sensitized to light with a chemical solution and whirled to dry evenly, is placed under the negative in a vacuum frame and exposed to powerful lights. Those areas of the plate exposed to the light become acid resistant, i.e., in the photo negative the line appears clear, permitting the passage of light. The white areas of the original art are opaque on the photo negative, blocking out the light. The metal plate is then developed and is ready for etching.

The plate is given a bath in a solution of nitric acid, which eats away the unprotected metal to a shallow depth, rinsed, and dried. After a number of procedures and processings (which are unnecessary to go into for our purpose) the plate is completed and ready for printing. The end result is a metal plate containing etched out areas, leaving in raised portions an exact replica, in reverse position, of the original art. These raised portions, when covered with ink and pressed to paper, will leave an identical impression of the original art—similar to the common rubber stamp (Figs. 94, 95, 96, and 97).

Fig. 92 Line art.

Fig. 93 Continuous tone art.

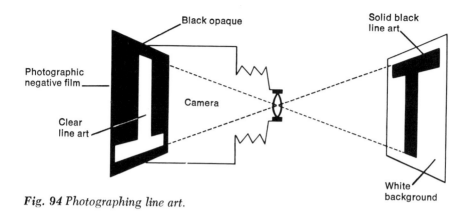

Fig. 94 *Photographing line art.*

Fig. 95 *Original line art.*

Fig. 96 *Line art printed from a line plate.*

Fig. 97 *Line plate (or cut) with the line in raised portions (relief.)*

CONTINUOUS TONE ART

A process similar to that used in the making of a line plate is followed with continuous tone art, except that a "screen" must be used in making the photographic negative. Printing is done with one color ink, not different values of that color. In order to achieve the effect or illusion of continuous tone, the art must be converted to a "halftone" plate.

The halftone plate is made by inserting a ruled screen between the camera lens and the sensitized film. The screen is made up of diagonal crosshatched lines, varying from fifty-five to one hundred fifty-five lines per square inch (a 55 screen, for example, contains 3,025 dots per square inch, etc.). Reflected light passing through the screeen breaks down the original art into various sized dots on the negative. In white and light areas on the plate, the dots are smaller than in dark and black areas. That is, just as the value changes from white to black, so does the size of the dots from small to large (Figs. 98, 99, and 100).

An example of halftone printing can be found in any daily newspaper. In viewing the picture at normal reading distance, note that the dot formation (screen) is unapparent. But upon closer examination (6" from the page or through a magnifying glass), you will be amazed to find that what appears to be a continuous blend of tones is really a maze of minute black dots of various sizes. Thus, printing with only *one color ink,* this screen creates the phenomenal optical illusion of continuous tone (Figs. 101 and 102).

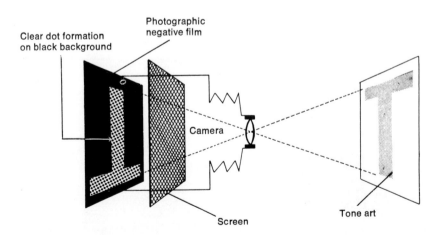

Fig. 98 Photographing continuous tone art.

Because of the variety of processes of platemaking, printing, and relative terminology, I will refer to the individuals involved in the three stages of platemaking, regardless of process, as follows:

Cameraman: photographs the mechanical or art

Film stripper: handles the films and negatives for plating

Platemaker: does the actual plating

Fig. 99 Here is a value change, from light to dark.

Fig. 100 Small dots in light areas get progressively larger until they merge into each other, creating the illusion of a white dot on black in the dark areas. (In the negative, the black dot is clear on a black background.)

Fig. 101 To the eye, this appears to be continuous tone.

Fig. 102 In reality, the art is a composite of dots of various sizes.

Fig. 103 This is 60 screen: *you can see the dots.*

Fig. 104 This is 85 screen: *the dots are less obvious.*

Fig. 105 This is 110 screen, *the image is much sharper.*

PHOTO RETOUCHING

With the exception of a few minor touches, the mechanical man is not usually required to retouch photos. However, a good board man should be able to do general retouching.

Because of the coarseness of newsprint paper, the dot (screen) must be coarse. A fine screen will blur or fill in when printed, causing a poor reproduction. The photo or artwork must, therefore, be coarse or retouched "hard;" i.e., a strong contrast of one value against the other. If the changes in value are blended or smooth, the coarse screen will lose much of the effect and detail, owing to the few large dots and spaces between the dots. However, if the changes are abrupt and of sharp tone contrast and have little detail, they will pick up in spite of the heavy dot. Newspapers generally use 50-65 screen. 85-110 screen is used in trade publications.

On the other hand, if the printing is being done on a slick magazine stock, a finer screen (100-120 screen, depending on the slickness of the stock) may be used. Under these conditions, the art or photo can be retouched with more detail and smooth blending of values. The dots in a finer screen, being smaller and more abundant, will pick up a better coverage of the areas, thus affording a truer reproduction. 120-133 screen is used on enamel and other smooth finished stocks, 150-175 on the highest coated only (Figs. 103, 104, and 105).

SQUARE HALFTONE

This is a plate (square or rectangular in shape) having right angle corners, with its entire surface carrying a dot formation (Fig. 106).

Fig. 106 In this image—a square halftone—there are no solid blacks or pure whites.

DROP-OUT HALFTONE (HIGHLIGHT HALFTONE)

In a normal halftone of an illustration containing white areas, for example, pure white areas or highlights will appear white but actually contain a fine dot (see Sihouette Halftone). In order to effect an actual white, these dots may be eliminated (dropped out) by the cameraman or film stripper (Figs. 107 and 108). This is much more effective in artwork than in photos. Drop-out in photos should be done with discretion, or the result may look very false.

Fig. 107 *Notice the dot formation in the white areas.*

Fig. 108 *In this drop-out halftone, the dots have been dropped out of the white areas.*

SILHOUETTE HALFTONE

If the original art is a shape on a white background and a square half-tone plate is made, the white background would not be pure white. It would pick up a minute dot called "papertone." If a pure white background is desired, the shape will have to be silhouetted so that just the unit itself will contain the screen with an abrupt ending of dots at the silhouetted edge, then printed onto white paper. This is done by the cameraman or the film stripper, who will mask or opaque (on the negative) the screen surrounding any part of the image (Figs. 109, 110, and 111).

Fig. 109 Here the original art has been rendered on a white background.

Fig. 110 *Reproduced in square halftone, this art looks as if it had been done on a gray background, an effect called "papertone."*

Fig. 111 *By silhouetting the image, the dot formation on the background and within the art area has been eliminated.*

VIGNETTE HALFTONE

A vignette halftone is a halftone blending into the paper along the edges, i.e., a gradual decrease in dot size until the dots disappear at the edges of the art and blend into the surface of the paper (Fig. 112).

Fig. 112 The vignette halftone produces soft edges that blend into the paper.

SCREENING

A screening is a mechanical application of dots, lines, or patterns used as a means of obtaining even values of black or color in conjunction with the line art (see Methods of Indication). (Figs. 113 and 114.)

Fig. 113 A line illustration in black and white.

Fig. 114 With a screened background, depth is added.

SURPRINT

In instances when line and halftone must appear as one unit, one super-imposed over the other, but the line and continuous tone originals are separate pieces of art, a *surprint* is employed. For example, the layout calls for tone art with a line of black type across it (Fig. 115). By combining the two negatives (line and halftone), the platemaker will produce one plate of this arrangement, thus producing this effect in one printing.

Surprint must be a combination of line and halftone or screen (tint) of the *same color*, i.e., black on gray, solid red on screen of red, solid green on a screen of green, etc. Solid red type on a gray photo or black type on a colored background are not examples of surprint because two separate color plates and printings are required. If the line of type were white, instead of black, it would be considered a drop-out.

Fig. 115 This is a surprint: line over tone.

COMBINATION PLATE

When continuous tone and line art are to appear together, but as separate elements, separate negatives are made (halftone and line) and are combined into one plate (Fig. 116).

this is a
COMBINATION

Fig. 116 A combination plate is made by combining tone and line art on one plate.

VELOX

If the cost of a halftone plate is too high to conform to the allocated budget, a method by which halftone effects may be achieved at a lower cost is employed. The original art is photographically converted to a halftone negative and printed onto a photographic paper in positive form called Velox. Because the Velox can be made to the required reproduction size and is composed of "line" dots, it may be placed in position on the mechanical to be used as finished art. The mechanical can then be shot completely in line.

Usually, the combined costs of Velox and line plates are less than the costs of a complete plate (line and halftone) made by the platemaker. This is especially true when silhouette and drop-out Veloxes are used.

In addition to the advantage of converting the continuous tone into halftone, the dots of the Velox can be retouched by the artist with white or black paint, or dropped out, or made into a combination of line and halftone by the Velox cameraman; thus, the artist has more control over the desired effects. Surprint Veloxes are obtainable, and Velox prints also come in nearly the same variety of screens as do metal plates. Line prints of type or drawings can be made instead of stats for better quality reproduction.

The term *Velox* in itself does not mean halftone. It is the name of the type of paper used. This paper can be used to make ordinary line prints as well as halftones. Therefore, the true terminology should be "Line" Velox and "Halftone" Velox, but this seems to create confusion. So a "Line" Velox is referred to simply as a Line print.

When using Veloxes for newspaper reproduction, you will notice that the reproduction proof has a tendency to be darker. In order to compensate for this fill in, the Velox should have a flat look; not as contrasty as you would expect it to appear in the paper. In such a case, instruct the Velox house to keep an "open dot."

DUPLICATING ADVERTISEMENTS

Frequently, the client will want to run the same ad in more than one newspaper at the same time. The various printing processes have different mechanical requirements in conjunction with preferred printing materials. In order to accommodate these requirements, printing seldom is done directly from the original metal engraving. Duplicates of an entire advertisement (including the type) are needed in order to run an advertisement in several different periodicals simultaneously if the printing process is letterpress. Many duplicate copies can be reproduced at a fraction of the cost of the original. One such substitute (to save time and expense) is the electrotype ("electro") made from the original engraving and used as the printing plate. Duplicate *molds* (called stereotype mats or matrices) can be made from this electro or directly from the original engraving.

These molds, made of a type of composition cardboard, are reasonably light and durable. They can be mailed or shipped to any part of the country, and duplicates of the original engraving can be made from them at a relatively low cost. The duplicates are made of a lead composition. In addition to the stereotype mat, a plastic mat also can be made which better serves the same purpose. Plastic plates are beginning to supplement the electrotype.

COLOR SEPARATION

Owing to the fact that only one color can be printed in the same area at a time, a *separate* plate must be made for *each color*. The component colors in a *full color* photo or art must be filtered and separated during the process of plate preparation in order that the correct proportion of each color can be obtained for each plate. This is called *process color* printing.

METHODS OF INDICATING COLOR SEPARATION

Art to be printed in two or more colors (other than process color) must be separated or indicated by the artist. The methods employed for indicating (defining) solid color and/or screen tints of color or black for the film stripper may vary according to the characteristics of the art and type of mechanical.

Examine the methods of indicating the art so that you can achieve the effects in Fig. 117. These methods apply whether the background is gray or color.

KEY OUTLINE

In this method of indicating color separation, the desired area is outlined with a thin red or black line directly in position on the art or mechanical with the line of type cemented in position. This thin red or black line acts as a guide for the film stripper (Fig. 118).

The outline itself is not retained in plating unless such is indicated. Black and red will photograph the same; however, of the two colors, red is more widely used. The reason obviously is the fact that, if a screen tint area is outlined in red, there is no question about whether or not the outline should be retained in plating, i.e., the reproduction will appear as a gray area with no outline.

On the other hand, if the area were outlined in black and no indication were made to delete this line on the negative, the area would appear when printed as gray with a black outline. If black outlines are to be used for such indications, they should be neatly "X'd" out with blue pencil or ink with instructions in the margin to indicate their deletion.

Fig. 117 This is the effect that is desired: black type over a gray background.

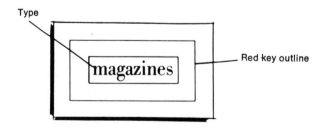

Fig. 118 In the key outline method, the desired area is outlined with a thin red or black line directly in position on the mechanical, the type cemented in position.

SOLID BLACK FILL-IN

In this method of indicating color separation, the area is filled in with solid black directly in position on the mechanical, and the line of type is cut out with a jagged edge and cemented in position (Fig. 119). In cutting the jagged edges, do not cut too close to the live matter. On the other hand, if the layout indicates a reverse or drop-out type in that area, a glossy negative stat of the type may be cemented into proper position (Fig. 120).

However, *only when stats are not available* for one reason or another may you prepare it as in Figs. 118 and 119 and indicate instructions for the line to be dropped out of the screen (Fig. 121). The positive may also be cemented onto a sheet of acetate or vellum taped over the mechanical. (See overlay.)

When type or art is to surprint or drop-out of a *halftone* instead of a screen tint, the same procedure is followed, i.e., using a matte stat of the halftone as a guide for size and position in the mechanical and cementing the line of type (cut out with a jagged edge) onto the stat in position or on an acetate overlay.

In shapes or areas of screen tint that may butt against a solid or another screen tint, a jagged edge of those shapes separating one from the other is used to retain the proper outline (Figs. 122 and 123). Butting one screen tint against the other should be done with discretion and the realization that the joining edges may create a moiré pattern or an irregular black line as a result of improper aligning of the rows of dots.

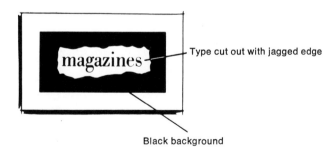

Type cut out with jagged edge

Black background

Fig. 119 In the solid black fill-in method of indicating color separation, the area is filled in with solid black directly in position on the mechanical, and the line of type is cut out with a jagged edge and cemented into position.

Glossy negative stat of type

Background completely filled in with black

Drop-out of screen

Fig. 121 This is the desired effect: type dropped out of screen.

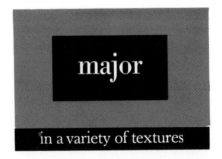

Fig. 122 In this instance, two screen values are being used.

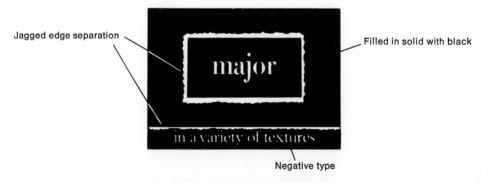

Jagged edge separation

Filled in solid with black

Negative type

Fig. 123 To prepare the mechanical for Fig. 122, butt one screen against another.

OVERLAY

In this method of indicating color separation, the shape may be outlined in light blue ink or pencil directly in position on the mechanical, and the line of type cemented in position (Fig. 124). Light blue will not pick up in the cameraman's negative; it is used as a visual guide. Then, a sheet of vellum or acetate, taped across the top, is placed over the mechanical. Registration marks must be drawn on the original mechanical in black ink outside the mechanical area, and corresponding marks accurately traced in ink on the overlay of vellum or acetate.

The outlined shape is then *completely* inked in with solid black on the overlay with no jagged edge (Fig. 125). If the line of type were to be dropped out of the background (as in Fig. 121), there would be no need for the overlay. This overlay acts as an individual mechanical for the color or screen tint area and automatically separates it from the type, which obviates a good deal of work for the film stripper.

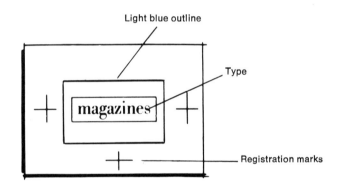

Fig. 124 In the overlay method of color separating, registration marks are a must.

Fig. 125 Ink the outlined shape completely with solid black on the overlay.

Fig. 126 Cut around the areas and shapes. Do not cut through the acetate.

Fig. 127 Peel away unwanted portions.

The corresponding blue outline is not always used in conjunction with the overlay; it is merely a precaution—a sort of belt and suspenders arrangement. Sometimes a red line is used for the same purpose.

A red color film sheet may be used in place of black ink on the overlay, scratching or cutting away the unwanted portions (outside the blue line). Red or deep orange films can be used for overlays because it photographs the same as black. Being translucent, this affords better visualization of the areas as they will appear in relation to one another. Each overlay *must* have registration marks to correspond with the art beneath it to insure perfect alignment of all elements.

Cover the art or mechanical with clear acetate. Then, using an adhesive color film, cut and peel away a section large enough to cover the area to be done. Lightly burnish it onto the clear acetate over the specific area. Cut around the areas and shapes (Fig. 126) and peel away the unwanted portions (Fig. 127). Then burnish in place. Use a clean razor blade or X-acto knife; a light pressure is all that is required to cut this film. After the excess is removed, there will be a residue of wax left on the acetate. It can be rubbed off with a clean, dry handkerchief. Do not use cotton for this.

A material that performs the same function but comes in another color is the ruby or amber colored film. This medium has a rubberlike coating on *acetate* that can be cut and peeled away, exposing the clear acetate. It is convenient because of the ease and cleanliness with which it can be handled. Both the ruby and amber photograph as black.

If you accidentally scratch or cut away a portion of the art, when working with color films or ruby and amber colored film, you can touch it up with black acetate ink. It may not look very neat, but these colors and black photograph the same. Actually, you can use a combination of adhesive color film or ruby colored film in conjunction with inking in of detail in black on the overlay, i.e., a job consisting of large masses as well as detail shapes can be done with this medium by using the ruby colored film as the entire overlay. Then cut and peel away the unwanted areas, including the entire portion that takes in the detail. Ink in the detail on the exposed acetate.

SELF-APPLIED SCREENING OR SHADING SHEETS

Among other widely used materials for achieving tints of color effects are textured commercial "shading" sheets. The film of desired texture or tint is placed in position on the mechanical or art and carefully cut out. The undesired areas are taken off, and the remaining portion is burnished in position (Figs. 128, 129, and 130). This eliminates much work for the film stripper, cuts down on the cost of the plate, and enables the artist to control the effects accordingly. An example of this method can be found in the cartoon section of any daily newspaper. Instructions for its use are clearly indicated on the sheet.

When working with self-applied shading sheets, little bubbles often appear on the surface as a result of air being trapped beneath. This will

Fig. 128 Here is the original art.

Fig. 129 Place the film over the art and cut.

Fig. 130 Burnish the sheet into position.

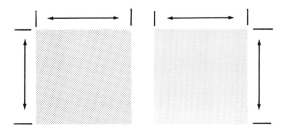

Fig. 131 Note the variations in values as a result of the number of dots per square inch.

interfere with reproduction. Puncture the bubbles lightly with a fine needle or push pin, then burnish gently to force the air out.

The surface of most shading sheets will accept ink in the event you have to do additional work in an area after it has been burnished into position. Try an acetate ink. The ink can conveniently be wiped off with wet cotton.

Some are confused by the different screen sizes used. All screen values in a 60 sc (coarse) have 60 dots to the linear inch. (There are 3,600 dots in 1 square inch.) The value change is a result of the dots being larger or smaller; in 110 sc (fine) there are 110 dots to the linear inch in each value, etc. (Here, there are 12,100 dots in 1 square inch.) The number of dots does not change with the value.

EXAMPLES OF APPLICATION

Fig. 132 represents a layout consisting of black type surprinting on a screen tint of black or color background and white type on a black background. Using the methods described above, the mechanical for this layout may be prepared in the ways shown in Figs. 133, 134, and 135.

At the completion of any such mechanical, a color guide (breakdown) must be made for the printer and platemaker. This is done by placing a tissue over the entire mechanical (taped across the top) and filling in the desired color shapes. On a black and white job, screen areas are usually indicated in *blue* but should be indicated in gray. Colored pencils or pastels may be used in color breakdowns.

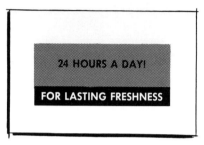

Fig. 132 Here is the desired effect: black type surprinting on a screen tint of black or color background and white type on a black background. This background can be a screen of black (gray), solid color, or a screen of color.

Fig. 133 Here is the indication with a key outline method.

Fig. 134 Here is the indication with solid black fill-in method.

Fig. 135 Here is the indication with the overlay method.

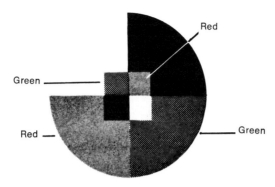

Fig. 136 Here is the desired effect: a three color mechanical.

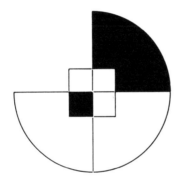

Fig. 137 Indications for color separation are indicated here with the key outline methods. Color areas are outlined in red.

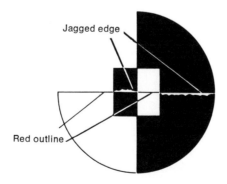

Fig. 138 Here is a combination of a solid black fill-in for one color and a key outline for the other color. Note: the jagged edge should appear only on one side. The edge of the completely filled-in side also acts as the edge of the color to butt against it.

Fig. 139 Here both colors are filled in solid black. Note the jagged edges.

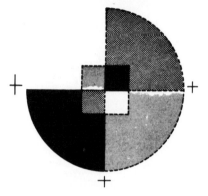

Fig. 140 Here the indication is made with one overlay and solid black fill-in. The black and green areas are filled in with solid black on the mechanical. The red areas are filled in with black on an acetate overlay.

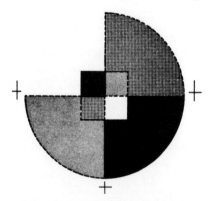

Fig. 141 This method employs two overlays. No jagged edge separation is needed. The black areas are filled in on the mechanical; the red areas are filled in with black on one overlay; the green areas are filled in with black on the second overlay.

Regardless of the method used, the end result from each mechanical will be identical. The method used depends upon the nature of the layout, means of reproduction, and costs involved.

Any combination of the same methods might be employed. The more colors involved, the more variations of separation can be worked out. For example, in a three color mechanical (black, green, and red) you might use any one of the approaches illustrated in Figs. 137 to 141 to obtain the required results. Fig. 136 represents the layout. Note that in all cases the *black* areas are always filled in solid. The *color of the key outline* has no bearing on the *color to be printed.*

5

Printing Processes

The following are the basic printing processes from which many methods of printing emanate. The purpose of this book is not to elaborate on production methods but simply to act as a vehicle of familiarization. More extensive studies may be made by referring to books on production in the list of reference books at the back of this book. These principles will supply you with the basics for understanding how the printed page is made.

LETTERPRESS (RELIEF PRINTING)

The printing surface (engraving), being raised, is covered with ink and pressed against the paper, thus transferring the image. Forms of relief printing surfaces include electrotypes, photoengravings, and type (Fig. 142). The majority of daily newspapers are printed in this method.

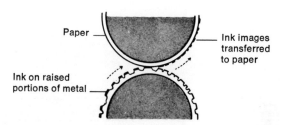

Fig. 142 This is the basis of letterpress printing.

GRAVURE (INTAGLIO)

The printing surface of the intaglio plate is the reverse of letterpress: its image is in the form of a depression rather than raised. The plate is covered with ink and wiped off, leaving ink deposits only in the depressions (or cells) of various depths. When the plate is pressed against the paper, the ink is sucked from these cells, leaving the image upon the surface of the paper. Examples of intaglio printing are photogravure and rotogravure (Fig. 143) which can be found in weekly supplements.

Fig. 143 This is the basis for intaglio (gravure) printing.

OFFSET (PLANOGRAPHIC PRINTING)

The surface of the plate in offset lithography is neither intaglio nor relief, but flat or planographic. However, the fact that water and grease do not mix is the principle of offset printing. The areas of the plate which are not to be printed are treated to give them an affinity to water. Before each printing, water is applied to the surface of the plate. The water repels the ink, which is greasy; the untreated areas retain the ink. In offset printing the plate does not transfer the image directly to the paper but to a rubber cylinder (mat) and then to the paper (Fig. 144).

In letterpress printing the type and/or "cuts" (engravings) are separate pieces and must be assembled for printing. This makes it possible to effect changes simply by replacing the particular cut or type (Fig. 145). In offset, the photographic negatives of type and art are assembled, and one complete printing plate is made from the negatives. Because each element is in its proper position as a single unit, it is impossible to effect a major change in the plate once it has been made. The same is true of intaglio printing (Fig. 146).

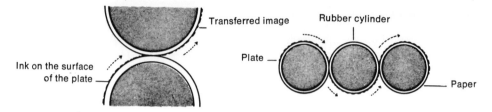

Ink on the surface of the plate — Transferred image

Rubber cylinder — Plate — Paper

Fig. 144 This is the basis for offset printing.

*Fig. 145 This is a letterpress form,
composed of separate pieces of metal.*

*Fig. 146 Unlike the letterpress plate,
the offset plate is a solid sheet.*

SILK SCREEN PRINTING

Silk screen is a process of printing through a stencil that is permanently affixed to a screen of silk (Fig. 147).

The open areas of the stencil permit paint to be forced through the exposed underlying screen mesh, while penetration of paint through the masked or blocked-out areas is impossible (Figs. 148 and 149).

The masked area, as a whole, may be prepared by using tusche, paper, old-fashioned block-outs, hand-cut film, or photographic film.

The screen mesh itself is made of a fine weave of silk, which permits an even flow and coverage of paint in printing. Silk is used because of its strength and durability.

Some of the advantages of this process are the achievement of brilliant color effects, the ability to print on difficult surfaces, the exclusion of expensive color plates, the ability to print on surfaces too large for standard printing presses, and the low cost in producing limited quantities.

Stencil

Frame

Open portions of stencil
exposing silk screen

*Fig. 147 In silk screen printing,
a stencil is affixed to a screen.*

Squeegee

Paint   Paper

*Fig. 148 A squeegee forces
the ink through the openings
in the stencil and screen.*

Printed image

Paper

Fig. 149 The end result of a silk screen print.

6

Folding and Trimming

In preparing mechanicals for pieces such as those described in this chapter, trim size and fold areas must be indicated. A *dash* line means fold; a *solid* line means trim (crop marks). These lines must be indicated in red or black ink on the mechanical outside of the trim edge and should not extend into the bleed area (Fig. 150). A thin blue line is often drawn around the trim edge as a visual aid.

BLEED

Bleed is employed in magazines, brochures, mailing pieces, posters, or any such printed piece that must be cut to a specific size or shape (die cut). When such a piece is designed to have "live matter" (art, color, tone, etc.) run off the edge, allowances must be made for the cutting process. For example, the dummy specifies that a band of color is to run along and off the bottom edge and both sides of a mailing piece (Fig. 151).

In making the mechanical you must indicate not just the actual coverage of the color, but an additional ⅛"—no less—from the trim edge wherever the color runs off the page (Fig. 152). This will provide extra color area in the event that the cutting should be somewhat inaccurate. If just the actual coverage were printed (stopping at the trim edge) and the cutting were off slightly, a white edge would appear, resulting in a poor effect. Therefore, this extra coverage or bleed is used as a precaution (Fig. 153).

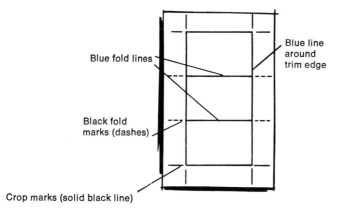

Blue fold lines

Blue line around trim edge

Black fold marks (dashes)

Crop marks (solid black line)

Fig. 150 *When preparing mechanicals, note the difference between fold marks and trim marks.*

Fig. 151 *The band of color runs off the edge of this piece: it is a bleed.*

⅛″ bleed of black

Fig. 152 *To indicate a bleed on the mechanical, carry the color an additional ⅛″ beyond the trim mark.*

Fig. 153 *If you neglect to carry the color beyond the trim mark, you may find an undesirable white edge appearing in the final piece.*

Fig. 154 *Study these folds. (A) ordinary booklet; (B) eight-page booklet; (C) four-page folder; (D) four-page letter; (E) six-page folder with short fold; (F) broadside with one short fold; (G) single-fold or two-fold card mailing piece; (H) French-fold; (I) eight page folder with short fold; (J) regular broadside; (K) two-fold mailing piece; (L) eight-page folder with two folds; (M) six-page folder.*

By the same token, if the layout calls for live matter to run very close to the edge, but not off (such as a line of type), be certain that you do not place it closer than permitted, according to the requirements of the printer. Should the type be too close to the edge and the cutting be off, the type also may be cut into.

Study the folds shown in Fig. 154.

7

Tricks of
the Trade

Now that the basics of the process of producing mechanicals have been described, here are some tricks of the trade which should be of use to you in particular assignments you may receive.

HOW TO USE A RULING PEN

In spite of his manual dexterity, the surgeon cannot perform efficiently with an inferior instrument. So it is with the artist and his tools. It has been said that a good artist can do a good job in spite of the condition of his equipment. This does *not* apply to the use of the ruling pen. The most skilled craftsman will have difficulty executing quality work if his pen is not in good condition. Likewise, a good tool in the hands of the incompetent will result both in inferior work and possible damage to the tool.

A good ruling pen is a prerequisite to efficient mechanicals. The most convenient type is the jackknife, or any such type that allows for proper cleaning. The less expensive pens are not of much use; they wear out quickly or do not rule clean lines. Your ruling pen should be kept clean while not in use. Never allow the ink to dry or form a crust around the point. If this should happen, clean it with ammonia or with water. Never scrape off dried ink or paint with a razor blade. Cleaning the pen frequently with water and a rag while it is in use will avoid stoppage of ink flow and broken lines.

These simple rules will insure professional and accurate results:

Fill the pen by using a dropper, placing it about ½" up from the point. Be careful not to overload the pen. *Never dip your pen into the ink.* Be

Fig. 155 Loading the ruling pen.

Fig. 156 Create a triangular space between the tip of the pen and the straightedge. Tilt the pen slightly back.

Fig. 157 Tilt the pen slightly to the side.

Fig. 158 If you tilt the pen forward, the ink will pull under the straightedge and blotch.

Fig. 159 If you tilt the pen too much to the side, you will get poor contact with the surface, resulting in inaccurate lines.

Fig. 160 Do not tilt the pen back too much. Not only will the contact be poor—consequently producing a poor line—but you will also damage the pen.

Fig. 161 Practice drawing lines of varying widths and lengths.

certain that the outside of the blades is clean before performing, or blotches and poor lines will result (Fig. 155).

Hold the pen with thumb and index finger in alignment with the second digit of the index finger—the screw adjustment facing out. Line up your straightedge directly on the pencil line. Now pull the straightedge away from the pencil line (about 1/32″).

Position the pen along the straightedge at a right angle to the surface, resting the last three fingers on the surface of the straightedge. Tilt it back and to the right *very slightly* so that the tip of the pen touches the pencil line. This will enable you to see the point without leaning over and also to create a triangular space between the tip of the pen and the straightedge (Figs. 156 and 157).

Slide the pen in this position along the edge without bending your wrist or elbow. *Do not press* the pen. The action should take place in the movement of your shoulders and arm as a unit. Never *push* your ruling pen. Whenever possible, the line to be drawn should be parallel to the shoulder line, even if it means turning the board or body. To obtain proper results, keep in mind that the direction of the stroke should be from left to right, or *away* from the body.

Do not tilt the pen forward. This will cause the ink to pull under the straightedge and blotch (Fig. 158). *Do not tilt* it back or to the side too far. Poor and inaccurate lines will result, in addition to wearing the points unevenly, subsequently destroying the efficiency of the pen (Figs. 159 and 160).

To prevent blotches and smears resulting from the pen in contact with the straightedge, some artists tape two pennies, or some other device, such as a triangle, blotter, etc., beneath the straightedge to lift the edge from the board. This is effective, but may scratch or damage the elements in the mechanical. Use with discretion. In order to get the feel of the ruling pen, it would help to experiment with the above rules. Practice drawing lines of various thicknesses and lengths in order that you may learn the limitations of your pen (Fig. 161).

Vertical lines should be ruled along the *left* side of a triangle. For one thing, the direction of light is from the left, permitting better vision of the line. More important is the fact that the line should be drawn parallel to the shoulder line (or reasonably so). Therefore, if you turn your body until your shoulders are parallel to the line, you will find that drawing the line on the left side of the triangle and away from the body can be done more efficiently and with greater freedom.

However, if drawn along the right edge, the stroke would be toward the body, causing a cramped position, and, too, there is a tendency to tip the pen forward in an attempt to see the line (which is in shadow). This causes blotting. Should it be *necessary* to draw a vertical line at the extreme right of the T-square, and drawing the vertical line along the *right edge* of the triangle is *unavoidable,* stand, lean over the board, and twist your left shoulder toward the line (your right shoulder away); then draw from *left to right.*

TEMPLATE PENS

There are a number of ink pens available that are unquestionably handy and much simpler to use than the ruling pen. However, the student should learn to use the ruling pen effectively rather than to rely completely upon the template pen. While it may be difficult to use at first, there are many problems that a ruling pen can solve much more effectively: it is several pens in one, inasmuch as you can control and change the weight of line in an instant, can draw on surfaces the template pen cannot draw on, and can be used for various colors of line without difficulty. Water paint or poster paint can be diluted enough to be used in the pen, very helpful when changes or revision of color line is necessary. Needless to say, a ruling pen line is probably the cleanest line possible.

Admittedly, though, this pen is difficult, if not often impossible to use with certain templates such as small ellipses, circles, etc. For these purposes, the template pen is, of course, your best tool. It should always be kept clean and in working order. Purchase a jar of pen cleaner or use ammonia to keep the nibs clean. If your budget permits, you can have one for red, blue, and black ink. The template pen is very useful in mechanical work.

USE OF BRUSH AND RULER

You will often have occasion to draw clean, straight lines on a painted surface, photograph, or surface that would cause a blurry or broken line if the ruling pen were used. A particularly useful method of producing clean lines under such conditions is to use the brush with the ruler.

For a straightedge, a *thick* metal-edged wooden ruler is preferable; a thin wooden or metal ruler is too flexible. With the left hand, hold the ruler metal-edge-up, and place it in position on the surface to be ruled on so that the thumb rests half on the bottom edge of the ruler, half on the surface, while the fingers overlap and the fingernails rest flat against the surface on the opposite side, permitting a firm grip. Drop the heel of the hand to the surface (Fig. 162).

Fig. 162 *Holding the ruler in this way, drop the heel of the hand to the board without touching the surface with your fingers.*

Fig. 163 *Hold the brush between the thumb and middle finger of the right hand, resting the index finger high on the ferrule.*

Fig. 164 *Place the remaining fingers behind the ferrule and against the thumb.*

Tip of thumb
on edge

Fig. 165 *Place the ferrule against the metal edge of the ruler so that the tip of the thumb rests upon this edge and the nail of the third finger lies flat against the front of the ruler.*

Fig. 166 *Practice using the brush and ruler with lines of varying lengths and widths.*

Hold the brush between the thumb and middle finger of the right hand, resting the index finger high on the ferrule (Fig. 163). Place the remaining fingers behind the ferrule and against the thumb (Fig. 164). Position the ferrule of the brush against the metal edge of the ruler so that the tip of the thumb rests upon this edge and the nail of the third finger lies flat against the front of the ruler (Fig. 165).

While some artists prefer to rest the nail of the middle finger against the ruler, I feel that the position just described affords a firmer grip. Some artists turn the hand slightly and rest just the tip of the thumb on the edge or side of the ruler, thus pressing the ferrule against the edge between the thumb and index finger.

Now, bring the brush into contact with the paper by pushing forward with the index and middle fingers. Move it along the edge, keeping an even pressure throughout. Keep the wrist high—do not twist it. To achieve a firm line, avoid too slow an action; develop a smooth, brisk stroke.

To vary the thickness of the line, simply vary the pressure of the fingers on the brush. The paint should be of a consistency just thin enough to flow freely from the brush.

Another advantage of this method is in silhouetting straight lines on photos when a pen might scratch the surface or deposit too heavy a layer of paint.

INKING

Clean corners are a *must* in inking. Whenever possible, draw the connecting line with the straightedge away from the adjoining line (Figs. 167 and 168). This will lessen the danger of pulling the ink under the straightedge, which would result in blotting.

Where heavy lines are needed (beyond the capacity of the pen in one stroke), it is best, if using the ruling pen, to build them up rather than to attempt them in one stroke (Fig. 169).

Sometimes a line is drawn too short and must be made longer. In that case, at the beginning of the connecting stroke, position the point above the paper and slightly to the left of the intersection. Then, with a sweeping motion, bring the pen into contact with the paper, blending one line into the other.

In drawing wide lines, it is sometimes best to ink in the outer edges and fill them in with a pen or brush. Do not make the outline too thin,

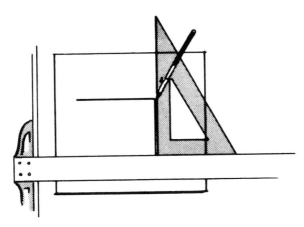

Fig. 167 Draw the connecting line with the straightedge away from the adjoining line.

Fig. 168 Do not place the triangle over the connecting line as shown here.

Fig. 169 If you want a thick line, build up the line with a succession of thin strikes with the ruling pen.

Fig. 170 *In drawing wide lines, it is sometimes best to ink in the outer edges and fill them in with a pen or brush.*

Fig. 171 *Do not make the outline too thin, or it may be difficult to paint up to it without going beyond.*

Fig. 172 *Fill in the lines with a brush or crowquill.*

Fig. 173 *Corners can be çrisscrossed, then touched up later with white paint.*

or it may be difficult to paint up to it without going beyond (Figs. 170 and 171).

To make corners with heavy or wide lines, draw a *thin* line to the point of the corner and build it up a little with a few more strokes; these additional strokes should *not* be drawn all the way. Then fill in with a brush or crowquill. This will prevent heavy blobs of ink deposits at the corners, thus avoiding blotching or round corners (Fig. 172).

Do not be afraid to use white paint to point up corners or lines. But do it *neatly*. Thick, sloppy patches of white paint do not necessarily interfere with the reproduction, but they give a very messy and unprofessional appearance. Some artists prefer to crisscross their corners and later sharpen them up with white paint (Fig. 173).

In the event that an inking job is smeared beyond repair, simply re-do it on a separate piece of paper (Strathmore), cut it out neatly, and cement it over the damaged area.

Should a line drawing of this nature have to be cut out, do not cut too close to the live edge unless it is unavoidable. Cutting too close to the edge may damage the line or cast a shadow during filming, resulting in a poor reproduction. All paste-up and cut marks will pick up on the negative and must be deleted by the film stripper before plating; if they are too close to the edge of the art, it is difficult for the opaquer to delete them.

DASH LINES

Measuring the dash and space precisely with a ruler is a tedious and often unnecessary time waster. Unless it is required, do not use this method.

Where just an effect is called for, you will save time and the results will be just as pleasing if you practice this simple approach.

Draw a continuous line; then, with white paint and brush, paint out the spaces by eye (Fig. 174). It may help to draw a dash at the beginning and one at the end of the line before starting. This helps to create a better illusion of evenness.

Your first attempt may not produce particularly good results. However, after a relatively short period of practice, your judgment will develop and surprising effects will begin to show.

Try this a few times: Draw a line about 3″ long. Decide upon the length of the dash and the space. Then proceed as described above. The last stroke of white should leave the last dash the correct length. Try several until you get the feel of it (Fig. 175). Now, draw two lines forming a right angle corner—and repeat (Fig. 176).

Fig. 174 *To make dashes, draw a continuous line, paint out the spaces in between. It helps to draw a dash at the beginning and at the end of the line before indicating the others.*

Fig. 175 *Dashes should appear equal.*

Fig. 176 *Working from left to right, draw two lines to indicate the corner.*

FREE HAND DASH

You may try drawing each dash with the pen rather than with the method just described. However, note that it is more difficult to control the over-all effect and that the dash is not as clean when drawn this way (Fig. 177).

— — — — —— — — — — — — — —

Fig. 177 Drawing the dashes freehand often produces uneven results.

ROUNDED CORNERS

Inking rounded corners can be troublesome if it is not approached in the proper manner. To begin with, unless the union of the straight line with the curve is exact, it will not look correct and will be difficult to rectify.

Using a 45° triangle, draw a diagonal line through A. If a 45° triangle is not available, pencil in the right angle corner as carefully as possible and construct a square within. Draw a diagonal through A-B (Fig. 178).

Positioning your pencil compass at an arbitrary point along this diagonal line, open until it touches the edge, and scribe a circle (Figs. 179 and 180). Repeat this, repositioning the point along the diagonal line until the desired curve is obtained. Using the same method, construct a diagonal line in each corner. Then, with the same compass setting, move the point of the compass along the diagonal line until the pencil point touches one side. Scribe the circle. Repeat this for each corner.

Now align your T-square with the center point and draw a light horizontal line from this point, intersecting the circle. With your triangle against the T-square and lined up with the center point, construct a light vertical line, intersecting the circle (Fig. 181).

Once the corners have been thus penciled, proceed to ink in—but ink in the curved lines first (Fig. 182), using the guide lines (Fig. 181) for the limit of the curve. It is easier to draw a straight line into or from a curve than to draw a curve into or from a straight line (Fig. 183).

Fig. 178 *To round corners, first draw a diagonal line through the right angle.*

Fig. 179 *Position one end of the compass on the diagonal line, the other on the edge of the square.*

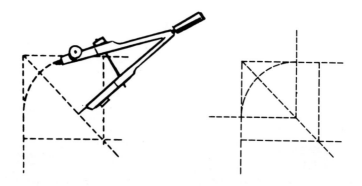

Fig. 180 *Draw the curve with the compass, being sure that it blends with the straight lines.*

Fig. 181 *Construct a light vertical line, intersecting the circle.*

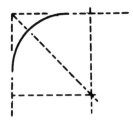

Fig. 182 *Ink in the curved lines first. Do not continue the inked line beyond the intersection.*

Fig. 183 *Draw the straight lines to or from the curved lines.*

Fig. 184 *Bad corner, due to inaccurate penciling.*

Fig. 185 *Bad corner results from impatience.*

Fig. 186 *Inaccurate inking produces bad corners.*

Although your penciling is worked out with a T-square and triangle, do not depend on these tools for the inking. There are many reasons why the lines may not match at the final inking. For one, the hole in the paper created by the compass point may widen, producing a broader swing of the compass; or, your hand may twist slightly while drawing the straight lines. Simply take a straightedge (triangle) and visually line it up so that the point of your pen (poise your pen in position slightly away from the surface) lines up with the intersection of the curve at both ends. Then ink in. If the line does not fall precisely on the pencil line, but blends into the curve, it will not be noticed.

The transfer sheet (or tracing sheet) is an aid to the artist for transferring shapes and drawings in the preparation of art and mechanicals. Ready-made sheets of various colors are available. However, you may prefer to prepare your own. Follow these directions:

Tape a sheet of tracing tissue onto the back of a pad (Fig. 187). Using a piece of pastel or graphite, rub from side to side, covering the entire sheet. Do not remove the excess pastel (Fig. 188).

With a ball of cotton (wet with thinner) smear neatly and lightly from side to side and top to bottom; re-wet if it dries out, but do not saturate the cotton (Fig. 189).

Repeat Figs. 188 and 189 two or three times until a good coating is obtained. Test the transfer sheet by placing a piece of paper over it and tracing a line. If the traced line on the back of this piece of paper is too light, give it another coat. Cut the tissue away from the cardboard, leaving about ½" of the tape on the tissue. This will provide the paper with a protective edge.

Fig. 187 *To make transfer paper, first tape a sheet of tracing tissue onto the back of a pad. The tissue must be flat.*

Fig. 188 *Without tearing the tissue, rub a piece of pastel or graphite from side to side until you cover the sheet.*

Fig. 189 Using a ball of cotton, wet with thinner, smear the surface lightly from side to side. Do not saturate the cotton.

FRENCH CURVE

Connecting curved lines requires precision and practice. The following is done if you are using a ruling pen, a template type pen not being available.

First, pencil in the curves accurately with your French curve. When ready to ink in, adjust the French curve until it is placed in the exact position of the pencil line. Then, pull slightly away from the pencil line, keeping a parallel gap between the pencil line and the edge of the French curve. In placing the ruling pen against the French curve, this little gap will dictate the *slight* backward tilt of the pen necessary for the point to touch the pencil line, thus creating the triangular space needed to avoid pulling the ink under the French curve and smearing (Fig. 190).

If your French curve has a beveled edge, the tilt back is not necessary. As an extra precaution, you may place a blotter beneath the French curve, raising it from the surface and lessening the danger of blotching. With the French curve properly positioned, check visually, lining up the pen with the beginning of the curve and its intersection with the next. Then ink in the first curve. Now, line up the French curve with the connecting line.

At the beginning of the connecting line, position the point above the paper and slightly to the left. Then, with a sweeping motion, bring the pen into contact with the paper, blending one line into the other. At the end or beginning of any ink line do not hold the pen in position. Learn to bring it *down* and *up* in a sweeping motion; otherwise, a ball of ink will form at the end of the line. If this should happen, you can, of course, clean it with poster paint (Figs. 191, 192, 193, and 194).

Fig. 190 *As you follow the pencil line with your ruling pen, pull the pen slightly away from the pencil line, keeping a parallel gap between the pencil line and the edge of the French curve.*

Fig. 191 *If two lines do not connect, as shown here, it is impossible to repair and must be done over.*

Fig. 192 *This is a common error, difficult to repair.*

Fig. 193 *This is a good intersection, but the lines are drawn too far. Clean with white paint.*

Fig. 194 *Connecting lines should look like this.*

BLACKENING EDGES

To blacken edges, some artists use a black grease crayon or felt tip pen. However, when cleaning with a pickup or applying thinner, it may smear, so use these with discretion.

Black ink or paint, applied with a crowquill or brush, is generally used for this purpose. The edges should be blackened before cementing into position. Blackening in after the piece has been cemented into position is both risky and troublesome. It is not always easy to clean the cement completely from the edge, which makes it difficult to apply the ink or paint.

A word of caution: use an old brush for blackening, because the sharpness of the paper edge will cut the hair on the brush. You may also slip and damage the art if the cut edge is very close. The safest and surest way is to hold the piece with the live matter facing away from the brush (Figs. 195 and 196). If you should slip, you will not impair the art. However, ink or paint may be cleaned off a photostat or photograph if it is wiped immediately with water and cotton.

Fig. 195 When blackening edges, do not hold the artwork facing toward you.

Fig. 196 Hold the art facing away from the brush, as shown here.

BLACK AREAS

For large areas of black on the mechanical or overlay, black paper is a time saver. First, ink in a clean outline and build up about ¼" width (Fig. 197). Then, cut a sheet of black colored paper to a size within that ¼", blacken the edges, and cement into the area (Fig. 198).

This will give complete coverage of the area with clean and accurate edges. It isn't always advisable to use the cut edge of the colored paper as the actual edge, for the simple reason that it may chip or peel. However, use the method you find best suited to the requirements of the layout.

In areas not large enough to bother using black paper, you may try filling in with black poster paint. Black paint dries in an even, flat black; it looks neater than ink and is better for reproduction. Additionally, rubber cement may be picked up with ease from a painted area, whereas cement has a tendency to adhere very firmly to ink, making it difficult to pick up. One word in the defense of ink—it is easier to touch up with white paint. Black paint does not work out too well on acetate—it has a tendency to crack and peel off, but it may be used in an emergency.

Fig. 197 To cover large areas of black on a mechanical or overlay, first ink in a clean outline, about ¼" wide.

Fig. 198 Then drop cement down a sheet of black paper to a size within that area and blacken the edges.

COLORED LINES

Lines that crisscross will spread slightly at the intersection. In lines of the same color this may not be too serious. On the other hand, where black and blue or red lines intersect, the black will run into the colored line if the colored line is drawn first (Fig. 199). If the black line is drawn, then the colored line, a clean joint will result (Fig. 200).

A most effective method when ruling colored lines is using poster paint rather than ink. Dilute the paint to a consistency that will permit it to flow freely from the pen. It will dry in even color and can be drawn over another color without a "see-through."

Fig. 199 *If the colored line is drawn first, the black will run into it and spread.*

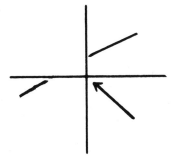

Fig. 200 *However, if the black line is drawn first, a clean joint will result.*

MOUNTING BUCKLED PHOTOS

Photos that are slightly curled or wrinkled can be mounted in the following manner. Cement both surfaces and allow them to dry. Using both hands, hold photo at either end and bend together (Fig. 201).

Place the curved edge onto the cemented board. *Roll* one side down (keeping the thumb pressed on upper surface to prevent buckling) and lightly burnish with the hand outward from the center (Fig. 202). Repeat with the other side.

Place a tissue over the photo and burnish outward from the center, forcing out the air creases. Rather than use the slipsheet method, this is also a quick method for mounting a photo that is not wrinkled but does not have to be placed accurately into position.

Photos that are severely buckled or wrinkled present a difficult problem for smooth mounting. Here is an effective method. First, cement the back of the photo and the mounting board and allow them to dry. Then, soak the photo in water until it becomes limp. While it is still wet, place it gently onto the dry cemented mounting board (as described in Figs. 201 and 202) and press firmly with a ball of wet cotton until all the air pockets and bubbles are gone. Be careful not to tear or scratch the emulsion. *Do not rub. Do not burnish until thoroughly dry.*

Fig. 201 To mount a curled or wrinkled photo, first hold the photo at either end and bend the edges together.

Fig. 202 *Roll down one side, keeping the thumbs pressed on the upper surface of the photo to prevent buckling.*

CUTTING

Whenever possible, cut along the outside edge of the needed piece. If the blade should slip, it will cut into the excess and not damage the area you are cutting out (Figs. 203 and 204).

In cutting a heavy board (illustration board), it is not necessary to apply too much pressure on the blade or knife in an attempt to cut through in one stroke. This is dangerous and usually produces an irregular edge. A few strokes of the blade, with an even pressure, will produce a clean, even cut. *Caution:* whenever possible, cut along the right-hand edge of the ruler. Never position yourself in such a way that you are criss-crossing hands while cutting. Besides making proper cutting difficult, it is obviously dangerous.

Fig. 203 *Do not cut art with the razor blade on the side of the art.*

Fig. 204 *Always cut with the blade on the side away from the art.*

CUTTING AND BUTTING

Here is a simple approach for butting or notching two or more elements (photos in this example).

The layout (Fig. 205) indicates that photo B is to notch into photo A. B and C are to butt flush. After assuring yourself that each photo will fit its respective shape, very carefully pencil in the shapes on the board.

Tape a tissue over the board and trace an accurate outline of the shapes. At this stage, you may also lightly trace the elements of each photo onto the tissue in proper position as a guide for pasting up and cropping. Use a soft pencil for tracing over photos. Cement the board and allow it to dry.

Cement photo A and, while it is still wet, place it in position beneath the tissue, lining up the photo with the tracing. You may use the dry slipsheet method if you prefer (Fig. 206).

Cut lines *1-2, 2-3.* Do not attempt to cut out the notched area of photo A (Fig. 207). Now paste up photo C in the same manner as A. Do not cut at this stage (Fig. 208).

Photo A beneath tissue

Shapes penciled on board and tissue

Fig. 205 Here is the layout: photo B *is to notch into photo* A. B *and* C *are to butt flush.*

Fig. 206 After tracing an accurate outline of the shapes, cement photo A *under the tissue, lining it up with the tracing.*

Fig. 207 *Cut out the lines, without cutting out the notched area of photo.*

Fig. 208 *Paste up photo C in the same manner. Do not cut tissue.*

Cement photo *B* into position overlapping *A* and *C* (Fig. 209). Double check to be certain that all edges overlap enough to insure clean butting after cutting. With a push pin, lightly pinpoint all the corners through the tissue and photos (Fig. 210). Lift the tissue and, with a steel edge and a sharp razor blade, line up the pinpoints and cut through both layers of photos (Fig. 211). In cutting, approach the corners with care. Do not cut beyond the corners, for the cut marks may mar the surrounding area.

Discard excess areas. Lift the remaining overlap, wet down the piece beneath it with thinner, and pull it out, dropping the overlap back into position (Figs. 212 and 213). Clean up excess rubber cement, rubbing *away* from the edges. Never erase or pickup in a direction toward the edge of the cemented piece or you might tear it (Fig. 214).

Another method employed by some artists is to eliminate the pinpointing and cut directly through the tracing and photos simultaneously.

Fig. 209 Cement photo B into position, overlapping A and C.

Fig. 210 Lightly pinpoint all the corners through the tissue and photos.

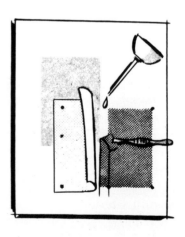

Fig. 211 After lifting the tissue, line up the pinpoints with a straightedge and cut through both layers of photos.

Fig. 212 Lift overlay, wet down the piece beneath it with thinner.

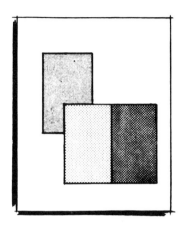

Fig. 213 Pull out the piece.
Be careful not to crack the photo
when lifting the corner.

Fig. 214 Clean up excess rubber cement.
Check edges for clean cuts and butting.

STRIPPING ILLUSTRATION BOARD

The surface of illustration board can be stripped from its cardboard backing, making it possible to effect changes in art, i.e., to transfer art to other surfaces without the thick backing or to gang up two or more pieces of art onto one board.

At a corner of the board, lift the surface away from the backing with a razor blade and pull it up about 1″ (Fig. 215). Place a clean cardboard cylinder diagonally across the lifted corner. Gripping the cylinder with both hands, press the loosened corner against the cylinder with the thumbs (Fig. 216).

Then roll the cylinder slowly and carefully until the entire piece is wrapped around it. Unroll it and, holding it face up at both ends, slide it lightly back and forth along the edge of your drawing table or any suitable smooth edge. This will relieve the piece of its curl (Fig. 217).

Before cementing a stripped piece, sand down the back to prevent impressions from showing through the surface. Press paper firmly with a free hand while sanding to prevent creasing or tearing. When sanding edges, sand out from the edge, being careful not to nick it. *Caution:* should the back of the surface begin to show while sanding—stop! You may cut through the surface.

Fig. 215 To strip illustration board, lift the surface away at the corner.

Fig. 216 Grip a cardboard cylinder with both hands, press the loosened corner against the cylinder with the thumbs.

Fig. 217 After rolling the cylinder until the entire piece is wrapped around it, slide the piece along the edge of the table.

USING GLUE

Pasting up small or tiny pieces of type, such as a number, a single letter, or patching a misspelled word is common practice in preparing mechanicals. The biggest problem is getting these small pieces to adhere firmly. If you use ordinary rubber cement, the piece generally picks up when removing the excess cement. This is especially true and rather disconcerting when working on acetate. One-coat cement is probably the most practical. Try using a dab of white or clear water soluble glue instead of rubber cement.

In preparing involved dummies, such as boxes or displays that require tabs and flaps, glue is much more satisfactory than rubber cement. This excess water soluble glue can be cleaned with a piece of damp cloth or cotton.

Mix a dab of this glue in with your water paint. It is excellent for painting on difficult or slick surfaces that may repel the water paint.

PREPARING LINE ART

If you are handling a complete job, illustration as well as mechanical, and you must prepare a line drawing, try drawing the art *repro size* if possible. The advantage here is that you will save time by not having to bother with photostats; the reproduction will be better because the art will be shot directly instead of from a stat; you will have better control in positioning it by working with it same size.

Familiarization with material and tools in conjunction with an understanding of reproduction is most important in your development as a professional. It leads to shortcuts, better results, and creativity. But when you prepare line art, do not be confused with gimmicks as the answer to your problems. Gimmicks often disguise themselves as the best way to do something because it is faster or easier. They usually stunt your development as a craftsman. There is nothing wrong with finding a shortcut or an easier way to produce a result, but do not lose sight of the fact that gimmicks, like drugs, only delude you into thinking that you are developing. Learn the difference between a mere trick and a legitimate solution.

The following exercises can be used as typical examples of what may frustrate the artist into using a gimmick, but these gimmicks prevent him from developing a skill necessary to produce a quality product. Before attempting these exercises, let's consider the possible approaches.

THE STAR

Suppose you had to produce a solid black or solid colored star.

Gimmick: find a picture of a star, have a negative photostat made to a larger size than required for reproduction and, with black and white ink or paint, clean it up. Have a positive stat made to correct size.

This serves the purpose, has limited use, and has not developed your ability. Suppose you had to produce the star in color? What would you do? Color the photostat? This may very well require the skill you have lacked in the first place.

Another gimmick would be to construct the star on black or colored paper and cut it out. You will get quick results but this method often produces frayed edges and poor reproduction, which are difficult to repair. These methods may help in the preparation of dummies and such, not for maturing of skills necessary for reproduction.

PROFESSIONAL APPROACH

Construct the star in pencil (Fig. 218). Ink it in with a ruling or template pen (Fig. 219).

If you have to produce a star in color, try using colored paint in your ruling pen. But, then again, you must know how to use the ruling pen.

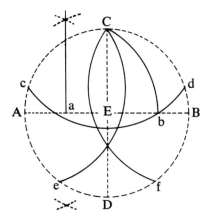

Fig. 218 Divide the circumference of a circle into four equal parts: A, B, C, and D. Label the center point E. Then divide A-E in half (point a); place the compass on point a and, opening it to C, draw arc Cb (b intersecting line EB). Then place the compass on point C and, extending it to the intersection b, scribe arc cbd (Fig. 1). With the compass placed at c and extended to C, scribe arc Ce; then place the compass on point d, extending it to C, and draw Cf.

Perhaps the best approach would be one really using ingenuity: construct the star in pencil. Cover the entire art with a piece of red adhesive color film (page 81). Then, carefully cut along the edges and remove the excess. The result will be far superior to any other method. The corners and points will be sharp and clean. The entire shape will be flat, with no danger of the edges fraying unless it is mishandled.

If you should fault during the performance, you can simply remove the film and start over or patch the area. The red color film will reproduce as if it were black ink.

If you had to construct a color star you would, of course, use that particular color film.

Also study the arrow, Fig. 220.

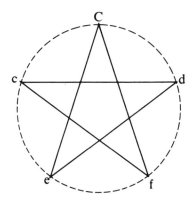

Fig. 219 Now connect Ce, Cf, cd, cf, de.

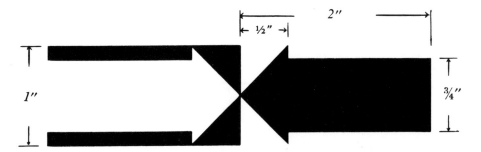

Fig. 220 Construct the above arrows following instructions as indicated. Keep the corners clean and sharp. Here is where your brush and ruler will be useful. Before inking, make a clean, accurate drawing. Notice what occurs at the meeting point of the two arrows after inking.

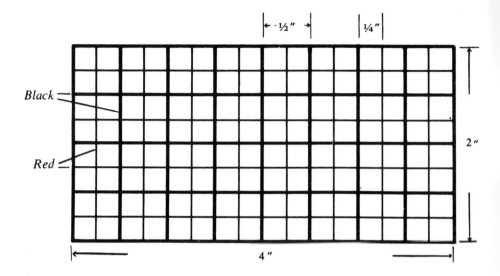

Fig. 221 *The illustration above is your layout. Follow it accurately. Be careful at the intersections—draw your black lines first. Follow layout for thicknesses of lines. Measure accurately and pencil in before inking. Heavy lines are blacks; thin lines are red.*

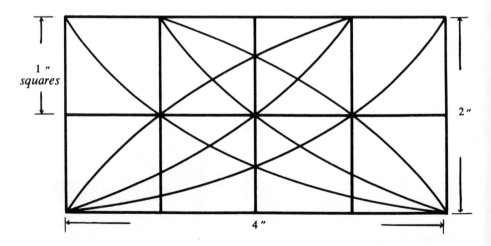

Fig. 222 *Your finished piece should look exactly like the layout above. The intersections must be precisely as shown.*

THE GRAPH

Now construct a graph. Gimmick: pencil the exercise as shown (Fig. 221). Use black and red tapes instead of ink. This method is fast but not professional, and it develops nothing for you. Of course, it is fine for presentation, layouts, dummies, and such, but we are concerned here with top quality mechanical preparation for reproduction. You'll also find this method can be more frustrating than if you had inked it in. It may be more difficult to get the tape straight than you might imagine. The crisscrosses and overlaps often produce poor results in reproduction.

PROFESSIONAL APPROACH

Use a ruling or a template pen for the black lines. Mix red paint so that it will flow freely from your ruling pen and proceed to rule the red lines directly over the black. This requires skill and can be used for similar projects. Also study the French curve, Fig. 222.

There are, of course, other possibilities but those just described may serve as a guide. Make an earnest attempt to do these exercises professionally.

8

Proportional Scaling

When art (photo, drawing, etc.) is not the actual size for reproduction and a lucy machine is not available, a scaling method may be employed to determine whether or not the art will fit the specifications (when reduced or enlarged) indicated in the layout.

Proportional scaling simply means that a shape, when reduced or enlarged in height, will proportionately reduce or enlarge in width, and vice versa. If we enlarge the 5″ side of a 5″ × 10″ rectangle to 15″ (3 times), then the 10″ side should increase in proportion—10″ × 3 = 30″ —with a total result of 15″ × 30″.

With the simple figures just described there is no problem. Nevertheless, there are times when the proportion of increase is not so easily ascertained. By using the method about to be described, you will have not only an accurate size, but also a quick visual of the shape in its new size, enabling you to change it immediately to suit your need without arithmetic or even a ruler.

DIAGONAL SCALING

There are occasions when there is no time to shoot a stat of the art to the desired size, or there may be so many pieces to be done that it would be impractical to shoot stats for a low budget job. In addition to scaling art, you will have to scale mechanicals to fit different page sizes. Each publication, newspaper, etc., has its own column and page size. If, for example, the client is running an ad in four different newspapers throughout the country, your mechanical should be prepared in scale to fit each of these specifications, or else a separate mechanical must be made for each size.

In scaling a rectangle or square, draw a diagonal line through *AB* (Fig. 223). In enlargements where desired height is known, mark off the height and draw a horizontal line from that point across until it meets the diagonal line (point *C*). This is, of course, an arbitrary point depending upon the height (Fig. 224). Drop a vertical line from that point to the extended base line *AD*. This will give you the width, at that height, in proportion (Fig. 225).

If enlargement on width is known, draw a vertical from that point to the diagonal and a horizontal across the intersection (Fig. 226). If reduction is required, the same procedure is employed, working within the shape (Fig. 227).

Drawing the above on a tissue and placing it over the art will afford you an excellent visual aid in determining where the art may be cropped.

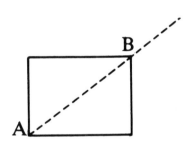

Fig. 223 In scaling, a rectangle or a square, draw a diagonal line through AB.

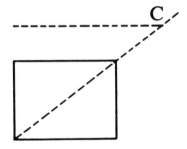

Fig. 224 Draw desired height as a horizontal line to intersect with diagonal.

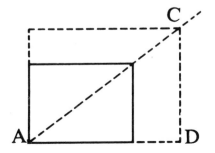

Fig. 225 From the intersection, drop a line to the extended base AD.

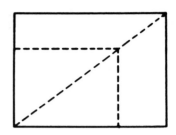

Fig. 226 Where the width is known, reverse the procedure.

Fig. 227 With reduction, use the same procedure, working within the shape.

SCALING IRREGULAR SHAPES

Construct a square or rectangle around the extremes of the shape (Figs. 228 and 229). Draw an infinite diagonal line through *AB*. Determine the over-all size required and follow the instructions above (Diagonal Scaling) to construct the square or rectangle, containing the original shape, in proportion (Fig. 230).

A diagonal line may be drawn from *A* through any point falling along lines *FB, BG* in order to project it to the determined size (*AECD*). In this case, the only point falling along *FB* is *a*. Draw *Aaa1* (Fig. 231). Point *b* falls on *BG*. Draw line *Abb1*.

To draw a diagonal line through a point *not* on line *FB* or *BG* in itself would conclude nothing. Two aspects of that point must be taken into consideration: its relative height and its relative position at that height.

Points *c* and *d* exist in space a certain distance up from *AG* and a certain distance in from *BG*. If you transfer *c* to line *BG* (*c1*) by drawing a horizontal through that point, you will have a point through which you may draw a diagonal line to *CD* (Fig. 232). Point *c2* represents the height of *c* in scale to *AECD*. Repeat the same for *d*.

Draw a diagonal line through points *c* and *d*. Now, draw a horizontal line across from *c2* and *d2* until it meets the diagonal just drawn. At their intersection you will find *c3*—or *c* in its relative position, and *d3*—or *d* in its relative position in scale (Fig. 233).

Any point along *AF* or *AG* must be transferred to its opposite line *BG* or *FB*. Therefore, a perpendicular from points *e* and *f* to line *FB* must be drawn, thus setting up points *e1* and *f1*, through which you may draw a diagonal to line *EC* (Fig. 234).

Now, simply drop *e2* and *f2* to line *AD* (Fig. 235). *e3* and *f3* now represent *e* and *f* in the same relative position in scale to *AECD*. Connect all plotted points (Fig. 236).

Remember: all diagonal lines must be drawn from *A* through a point existing in space and/or through a point only on lines *FB* or *BG*.

Now and then the layout will consist of many photos or art (as in a catalog, brochure, etc.). The cost of statting many photos may be too high for the job. Therefore, by using the diagonal system, you will be able to recreate the shape proportionately to any size larger or smaller to accommodate the original art. Once the size and shape are ascertained, cut it out of a sheet of heavy bond, place it over the art in proper position, and tape it across the top. This is called a "mask" (Fig. 237).

On the mechanical, the actual shape (reproduction size) is drawn in a blue line and keyed (*A-B*, etc.) to correspond with the art. The masked art will present an excellent visual of how the art fits into that particular shape.

Fig. 228 *The problem is to scale this irregular shape.*

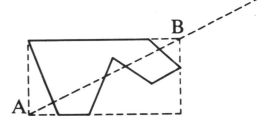

Fig. 229 *Construct a square or rectangle around the extremes of the shape.*

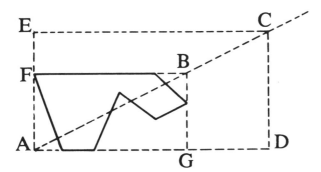

Fig. 230 *Enlarge the over-all size in the same way you would a square or rectangle.*

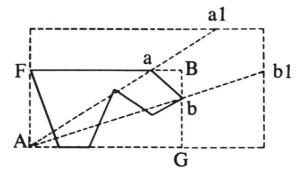

Fig. 231 Projecting and establishing line ab.

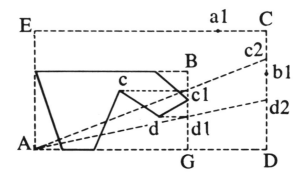

Fig. 232 Projecting line cd.

Fig. 233 Establishing cd.

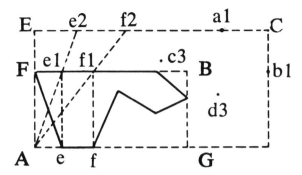

Fig. 234 Projecting line ef.

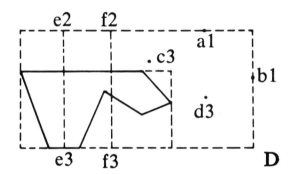

Fig. 235 Establishing line ef.

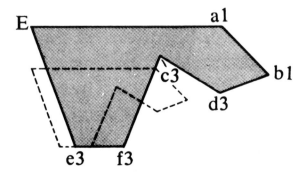

Fig. 236 Here is the new size in proportion.

Fig. 237 *A mask can be used to indicate a new size when photostats are not available.*

EXERCISE

Trace the shape in Fig. 238 and enlarge it proportionately from height A to height B. Using different colored pencils for identification of plotting lines may simplify this procedure. After having drawn the shape to its new size, try cutting it out of a piece of heavy bond.

There will be occasions when you will have to cut a mask for a photo or art to correspond in proportion to a particular shape in a layout. By applying the principles just covered, you will be able to plot any shape to any size, larger or smaller, in correct proportion.

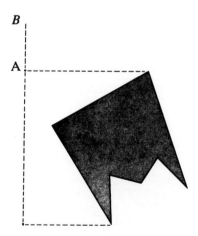

Fig. 238 *Enlarge this shape proportionately from height* A *to height* B.

PROPORTIONAL SLIDE RULE

For simple shapes (triangle, square, etc.) that must be enlarged considerably (as in posters, presentations, etc.) and where the diagonal line system is physically impractical, the fastest and surest method is to use a proportional slide rule.

For example, if the original art measures 7″ wide by 10″ high and it must be enlarged to 40″ high, you must be concerned with how wide it will have to be at this height to be in proportion. Since the height must be increased four times, the solution is simple: multiply the width (7″ by 4 = 28″. So, the over-all size would be 28″ by 40″. But should the measurements be uneven numbers—$7\frac{3}{16}$″ × $10\frac{5}{8}$″—and the enlargement an odd size—$37\frac{15}{16}$″—the percentage of enlargement becomes more difficult to ascertain. Therefore, the proportional slide rule should be used. Instructions for its use are clearly indicated on the instrument. The mathematical formula for proportion:

Width is to width as height is to height, i.e., $\dfrac{7''}{x} = \dfrac{10''}{40''} = 10x\overset{28''}{\overline{)280}}$

SPACING

How to divide odd-sized areas into equal spaces is an important thing to know, especially in the preparation of charts and graphs. A fast and accurate system is, once again, the principle of the diagonal approach.

As an example, we will use an area $7\frac{3}{16}$″ wide by $3\frac{1}{8}$″ high. The width is to be divided into six equal spaces, the height into five. In order to divide the height into five equal spaces, first pencil in the over-all shape. Place the 0 mark of your ruler at the lower left-hand corner. Pivoting the ruler at this point, swing it until the 5″ mark touches the *top horizontal line* (Fig. 239).

If the 5″ mark goes beyond the original shape, simply extend the top line and swing the ruler until it meets it (Fig. 240). If the 5″ mark does not reach the top line, i.e., if the space is too wide, calculate an equal multiple of 5″ that will reach it—10″, for example, counting every other inch as one.

Once the diagonal position has been attained, hold your ruler firmly and draw a light line along the edge. Now, ruler still in place, mark off the five equal points (Fig. 241). Draw a *horizontal* line through each point with your T-square (Fig. 242).

In order to determine the division of the *width*, place the end of your ruler in the lower left-hand corner and pivot it until the 6″ mark touches the *opposite vertical* (Fig. 243).

Follow the same procedure as just described for the height, with one exception: draw *vertical* lines through the points (Fig. 244).

This is one of the methods used in plotting charts and graphs, as well as preparing mechanicals that need particular spacing of shapes and areas. A helpful device in calculating spaces is the engineer's scale rule.

Fig. 239 *To divide odd-sized areas into five equal spaces; first pivot the ruler from the lower left-hand corner until the 5″ mark touches the top horizontal line.*

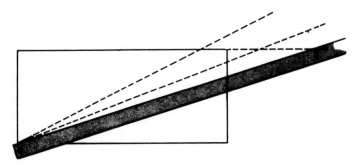

Fig. 240 *If necessary, extend the top line to meet the 5″ mark.*

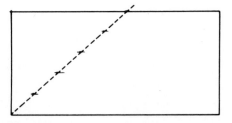

Fig. 241 *Draw a diagonal and divide that diagonal into five equal points.*

Fig. 242 *Using your T-square, draw off five horizontal lines.*

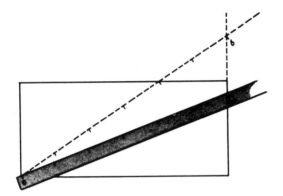

Fig. 243 *To divide the width into six equal parts, pivot the ruler along the opposite vertical.*

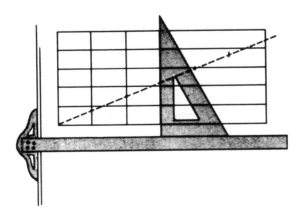

Fig. 244 *Drawing vertical lines through the points, follow the same procedure as before.*

EXERCISE

Divide a rectangle 8⅝″ wide by 4¹³⁄₁₆″ high into 10 equal horizontal spaces and 13 equal vertical spaces (Fig. 245).

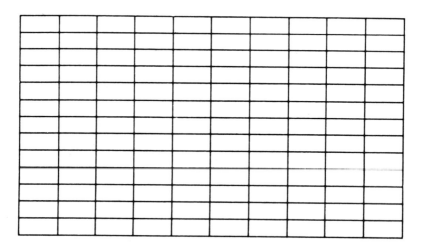

Fig. 245 Divide a rectangle in this proportion into ten equal horizontal spaces and thirteen equal vertical spaces.

CONSIDERING THE TIME FACTOR

One important aspect of advertising should not be overlooked: the element of time. As a general rule, a job should be completed as quickly as possible. On many occasions, there is very little time in which to execute a mechanical. Time sheets or some other sort of record are accurately kept of the work entailed during a project. This system is not necessarily employed to check on the artist's capabilities, but as a means of estimating the cost for billing the client.

Obviously, the faster the artist, the more valuable he becomes to the organization. But do not overlook the fact that speed comes from knowledge and experience. Working fast, without forethought, may result in a mass of confusion and errors, jeopardizing the reputation of the agency or studio *as well as your position.*

Rather than rush frantically and furiously into a mechanical, simply study its requirements. Then decide how you should approach its execution. If you know the information covered in this book, the performance will not take any longer than is necessary.

9

How to Execute
a Mechanical

Each layout has its own significant characteristics. The approach and method of preparing a mechanical is relative to these characteristics and to the different working procedures in each agency and studio. In order to prepare a mechanical easily and efficiently, it is necessary not only to understand the information just covered, but also to develop an approach to its analysis and execution. Because of this, there is no rule of approach. Each artist has his particular way of handling a mechanical; nevertheless, I have outlined here a general approach applicable to most situations through which you may develop your own methods.

STEP ONE

Analyze the layout or dummy (Fig. 246) and *ask questions*. Never start a mechanical without having a thorough understanding of its requirements:

(a) How is it to be used—as a mailing piece, newspaper ad, magazine page, etc.?

(b) A black and white job, two-color, or multicolor?

(c) Any halftones (art or photos)?

(d) What size is the mechanical to be? Any bleed areas or folds?

(e) If die cutting is involved, check the shape.

(f) Does the type fit the layout?

(g) Will you need photostats or Veloxes? Any silhouetting?

(h) Reverse copy? Surprint?

(i) If screen tints or color separation is needed, what method is to be used—key outline, solid black on board, overlays, color film sheet?

(j) How much time is available?

Once these questions have been resolved by your art director, production manager, or supervisor, you may start the mechanical.

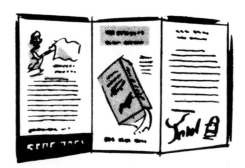

Fig. 246 Study the layout.

STEP TWO

Fix or powder the type proofs to prevent smearing (Fig. 247). Keep a clean cutting board on hand, a back of a pad, for example. Most artists prefer to cement the back of the entire proof (Fig. 248), allow it to dry, place it (back down) onto the cutting board, and cut out all the type areas with a razor blade and steel T-square, leaving them in place on the board (Fig. 249). Then, as each piece is needed, it is lifted and used.

This method, of course, is the most practical because it minimizes handling of the type, keeps the cemented area clean, and produces a neater cutting job. It also prevents cement from wetting and smearing the type, which would occur if pieces were individually cut and then cemented.

Never cut with a good plastic T-square or triangle; one nick will ruin its efficiency for inking work. If a steel triangle is not available, keep on hand a particular triangle to be used just for cutting. Aluminum or magnesium tools are dangerous for cutting. They are too soft; the blade often catches and rides up.

Fig. 247 Fix or powder the type proofs.

Fig. 248 *You can cement the back of the type proofs if you like.*

Cutting board

Type proof

Fig. 249 *Cut out the type squarely, using a T-square.*

STEP THREE

As a time saver, order your stats (if any) before starting the mechanical, being certain of correct sizes. While you are preparing the mechanical, your stats are being made. If the stats are ordered after you have gone as far as you can with the execution of the mechanical, it will mean a delay while waiting for them. Time is vitally important and costly in business (Fig. 250).

Fig. 250 Gang up the art for photostats.

STEP FOUR

Set up your board. Cut the illustration board about 2″ or 3″ larger than the mechanical size to allow a comfortable margin for written instructions. *Never* use pebbled matboard for a mechanical. If the layout calls for any amount of inking, be certain to use a smooth surface illustration board for cleaner lines. Where textured effects are required in inking, use the medium or rough surface illustration board.

Now "square up" your board. Position your board on the left of the drawing table, being certain not to overlap the straight edge of the drawing table. This will allow some working space at your right and will afford better results in using your T-square and triangle. If you are left-handed, reverse this procedure.

Holding your T-square firmly in position at the bottom of the drawing table, line up the lower edge of the board against it. *Tack* it down at the top corners. Tape isn't particularly useful because of its tendency to pull or slip out of position (Fig. 251).

With T-square and triangle, pencil in the over-all required size of the mechanical (visually centered). For most accurate and clean penciling, use a 5H or 6H pencil with a long sharp point (use your sand block). This will minimize excess graphite smudges caused by the use of softer pencils. Do not press too hard, or you may damage the surface of the board (which, subsequently, will cause poor inking). Cleanliness and accuracy are the hallmarks of a professional mechanical.

Caution: the beginner has a tendency to dig his pencil into the board while marking off sizes. This will cause holes in the board or paper and perhaps result in a poor inking job.

Fig. 251 Tack down the illustration board so that it is square.

STEP FIVE

Once the over-all size has been lightly penciled in, *ink in crop marks and/or fold marks* where and if required as well as fold lines and trim lines (shown as dashed lines in Figs. 252, 253, 254, but should be continuous light blue lines. See page 92). This will insure the retention of sizes and areas in the event that the penciling is erased during the process of pasting up (Fig. 252). It will also serve as a means of checking, as you progress, the squareness of the mechanical. Now pencil in the entire mechanical, areas to be screened, etc. *Do not ink in yet* (Fig. 253).

Fold marks (short dashes)

Crop marks
(single dashes)

Fig. 252 Mark off the crop and fold marks as well as fold and trim lines.

Screen area
(plus bleed at top)

Solid black area
(plus bleed left and bottom)

Fig. 253 Indicate the areas to be screened.

top-rated

Fig. 254 Clean broken type.

STEP SIX

Check type, using the glassine on top of the mechanical and elements to be pasted in, being certain that they fit properly in accordance with the layout. Also scrutinize the type for broken letters or smears (Fig. 254).

Check sizes of shapes, photos, art, bleed areas, etc. You will often find that the elements to be assembled in the mechanical do not fit precisely as indicated in the layout. Should the difference in size be considerable, bring it to the attention of your art director, or whoever is in charge of the project. He will suggest the necessary changes. If the difference is slight, use your own judgment in arranging the elements to resemble the layout as closely as possible. Remember, often the layout is done free hand. It merely represents the "effect" the art director has in mind.

STEP SEVEN

Once these questions have been resolved, ink in the required areas (Fig. 255). If, as often occurs with the beginner, the elements are cemented in before inking, the chances of scratching, dirtying, or dropping ink onto the type or art are very likely to be increased. This may mean doing the entire mechanical over or manipulating extensively to rectify the condition; whereas, if the inking is executed before cementing in the type or art, and an error in inking is encountered (spilling, blotching, wrong size, etc.), it will minimize the danger to the components. In addition to this, there is less danger of smudging or scratching the pasted elements as a result of manipulation of the T-square and triangle. Accuracy of size, shape, and squareness of your mechanical is of prime importance.

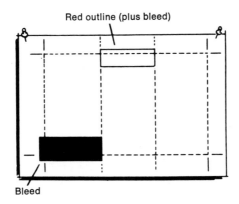

Fig. 255 Ink in the required areas.

STEP EIGHT

Commence paste-up (Fig. 256). Usually, by the time your stats arrive, a good portion (if not all) of the mechanical will have been completed. This depends upon the complexity of the job. Check the stats for proper size and positioning. If all is in order, continue the mechanical (Figs. 257 and 258).

Fig. 256 Begin the paste-up.

Fig. 257 The mechanical is completed.

Fig. 258 The page will look something like this after it is printed, trimmed, and ready to be folded.

STEP NINE

At the completion of the job, you should double check against the dummy or layout, being certain that all elements are the correct size and in their proper position. Using red ink, "X" out each photostat of continuous tone art and indicate in the margin: "Stats for size and position only. Strip in original art." The line (glossy) stats should *not* be "X'd" out, as they would more than likely be used for finished art.

Next, pick up excess rubber cement and clean with a good eraser. Required instructions, sizes, job number, etc., should be written in the margin. If screen or color indications are required, tape a sheet of tracing paper across the top covering the entire board and indicate the requirements. A tracing paper or vellum cover is also convenient for written instructions or indicated changes (Fig. 259). In addition to the tissue flap, a heavier paper flap is cemented about 3" along the top of the reverse side of the board and flapped over the front for decor and protection (Fig. 260).

The mechanical, along with the dummy or layout and art, should then be presented to your supervisor for final checking (Fig. 261).

Fig. 259 *Using an overlay for protection and for written instructions is always a good idea.*

Fig. 260 *A heavier flap—about 3" wide—is cemented along the top of the reverse side of the board.*

Fig. 261 *All elements are presented: art, layout, and mechanicals.*

10

Variations of Layouts and Mechanicals

To exercise some of the information previously covered, let us now discuss typical layouts and approaches to their mechanical assembly.

The layouts discussed in this chapter are not to be judged for their quality of design. They are merely practice arrangements for the sake of exercising some of the information covered in this book. In some cases, there may be more variations than covered here, but I feel it unnecessary to carry them any further.

COMBINATION WITH SURPRINT

Cement the body type in position on the mechanical. There are several methods for preparing a surprint half-tone; for example:

A stat of the original continuous tone art may be cemented in position on the mechanical. The surprinting line of type may be cut out with a jagged edge and cemented into proper position directly on the stat. With red ink, "X" out the stat and write in the margin: "Stat for size and position only. Strip in original art; surprint this type in position."

Instructions can be written either in the margin around the mechanical or on a tissue flap, or both. Instructions for screening the art should be clearly indicated on the art: "65 sc. sq. halftone with surprint. Follow mechanical for size, position, and surprint (for letterpress)." The art is sent along with the mechanical for plating.

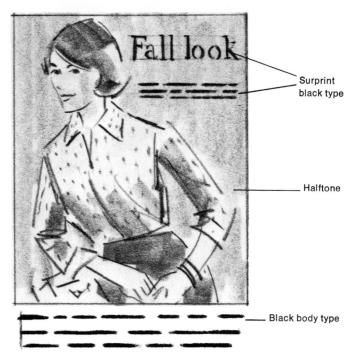

Fig. 262 Combination with surprint.

Should the original continuous tone art be the same size (s/s) as indicated in the layout (and if physically possible) it can be cemented directly in position on the mechanical. The line of type, however, cannot be cemented on top of the art for the simple reason that the art will be screened directly and the type proof paper will block out that portion of the art, i.e., the end result would be a halftone with black type surrounded by a white jagged edged shape.

To prepare this art, therefore, paste up the type on an acetate overlay along with the body copy. It is more practical to keep all the line copy together on one board or overlay. Should the line copy be in a large quantity and of such a nature as to require extensive manipulation or handling, it might be best to reverse the procedure, placing all the line type on the board and the tone art on the overlay.

Instructions for the original art might read, "s/s 65 sc. sq. halftone—surprint type as indicated (for letterpress)."

A less expensive approach would be to use a Velox print for the surprint halftone. The preparation of copy for Velox is generally the same as for plating. Either of the above methods may be employed, for example, the type is cut out with a jagged edge and cemented on a stat of the original art. Both the stat arrangement and the original art are sent to the Velox house. The same instructions are indicated as on the mechanical.

If the original art is s/s, the type can be placed on an overlay taped over it. Should the original be larger or smaller than reproduction size, simply enlarge or reduce the type by photostat to accommodate the art.

When the surprint Velox is received, cement it into position on the mechanical along with the body copy. The end result is a mechanical containing all "line copy."

COMBINATION WITH DROP-OUT

Apply the same procedure as for "Combination With Surprint." However, an additional variation may be followed: use negative type instead of positive for the drop-out, along with the written instructions for drop-out instead of surprint.

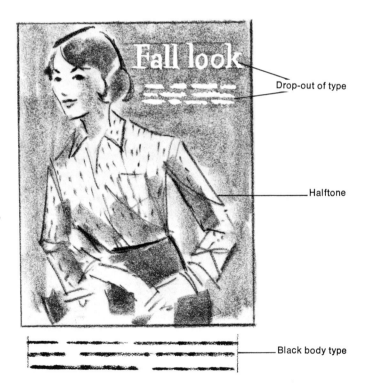

Fig. 263 Combination with drop-out.

TWO COLOR LINE (BLACK AND COLOR)

If the line drawing is s/s, cement it in position along with the body type and signature. If not, use a glossy stat.

Prepare an acetate overlay for the second color. Blacken in the second color areas of the line drawing and paste up the headline and reverse logo. On the overlay, write "100% Green Plate" (or whatever color is required). On the board, write "Black Plate." On a tissue overlay, fill in the color areas with pencil or pastel of the desired color.

Often the original drawing is made larger and the overlay prepared on the art to that size. In this case, you may use a matte stat of the original (shot through the overlay) and paste it on the mechanical for size and position. The only elements on the overlay for the mechanical itself would be, in this case, headline and reverse logo. Send both the original art and mechanical to the platemaker.

An overlay for the second color was used here because of the complex

Fig. 264 Two color line (black and color).

nature of the artwork, which made it difficult to use the "key outline" or "solid black fill-in" method directly in position on the art. However, when the design of the art is such that a red key outline can be used and the additional color elements in the layout are independent of the black areas, the entire mechanical can be prepared without an overlay. The cameraman will shoot the mechanical twice, and the film stripper will separate the color elements on his negatives in accordance with your instructions.

TWO COLOR COMBINATION

Here, by two color combination is meant a color with black line, halftone, and screen tint, second color line with screen tint.

Paste up the all black elements on the board: the two line spots (probably glossy stats), body copy, and signature. The screen tint surprint area may be handled in one of two ways: either a red key outline

Black line and color area

Surprint black type over screen

Color shape

Black halftone with line and screen color areas

Black body type

Color headline

Color logo

Black signature

Fig. 265 Two color combination (with black, line, halftone and screen, second color line with screen).

and black type cemented in position or solid black fill-ins with black type (cut out with a jagged edge) in position.

Once again, depending upon the nature and complexity of the original continuous tone art, several approaches for its mechanical assembly are possible.

For the sake of simplification, assume the art to be a wash drawing with certain areas to be over printed in solid and screen of color and larger than reproduction size. Prepare it as a separate unit, i.e., the original wash drawing with an overlay for the second color, regardless of size.

The col reas on the overlay are to be filled in with solid black. If areas of solid color butt against a screen, they should be separated with a jagged edge or done on another overlay. A red color film sheet could be used for the overlay, rather than black on acetate, making it easier to visualize the effect. If the art is prepared in this manner, shoot a matte stat of it (through the overlay), paste it in position on the mechanical, and "X" it out in red ink.

The same procedure applies to the black line spots and stats of the art to be cemented into the mechanical for relative size and position. The original art is sent to the platemaker along with the mechanical.

Rather than prepare the art as separate units, it may be more practical to prepare each piece s/s in position on the mechanical, perhaps using glossy stats of the line drawings and a halftone Velox of the wash drawings. This will simplify the job, because an overlay for the second color can be prepared as one unit, i.e., the art shapes, logo, and headline all on one overlay.

Draw the curved line in solid black on the overlay. Now, on a tracing tissue overlay, indicate with colored pencil (reasonably close to the desired printing color) the color areas, making a notation for the screen shapes.

With pencil, gray pastel, or felt tip marker, fill in on the tissue the screen of *black*. Be certain to indicate the percentages of screen tints.

Do not rely on these simple examples alone. Study magazines and newspaper advertisements; look more professionally at the mailing pieces you receive at home. Ask yourself how you would have prepared the mechanical for this ad, or how was a particular effect achieved? Why did the designer approach it this way, why not another arrangement? Perhaps his budget prevented the use of screens or second color which might have helped; or the simplicity of an approach and intelligent use of available facilities may be the very thing that makes a particular ad outstanding. Remember: the *effect* is the result of *advertising knowhow*.

Black surprint

Black headline

Halftone

Color arrow

Line spot in color

Black body type

Black logo

Color type

Black line spot and screen of color

Screen of black

Line of type half dropped out of halftone, the rest black

Fig. 266 Analyze this one on your own.

Index

New edition edited by Susan E. Meyer
Designed by James Craig and Bob Fillie
Composed in 10 point Caledonia by Atlantic Linotype Corp.
Printed and bound by Halliday Lithograph Corp.